Social, Civil, and Savvy

Training & Socializing Puppies to Become the Best Possible Dogs

Laura VanArendonk Baugh
CPDT-KA KPACTP

Æclipse Press
Indianapolis, IN

Copyright 2017 Laura VanArendonk Baugh
Cover design by Laura VanArendonk Baugh and Alena Van Arendonk
Illustrations by ZJ Bickel
Author photo by Elemental Photography
Interior photos page 126 by Alena Van Arendonk
Interior photos page 145 by Nancy VanArendonk
Cover photos and interior photos pages 1, 13, 21, 35, 47, 79, 65, 101, 109, 119, 131, 137 by DepositPhotos
Interior photos page 38, by Fotolia
Interior photos pages 26, 93 by Laura VanArendonk Baugh
Technical review by Casey Lomonaco

ISBN 978-1-63165-006-2

www.Aeclipse-Press.com

About this book

Whatever else my faults, I raise fearless puppies.

I realized this first when I was walking my guide-dog-in-training around Gen Con, one of the world's largest geeky conventions. The event has about 65,000 attendees and quarters are crowded, participants often brushing shoulder to shoulder. Amidst the crowd we passed a dancing Big Bird, a man on stilts, a mobile and conversing Dalek, and a fairly good recreation of Captain Davy Jones from the *Pirates of the Caribbean* film franchise, complete with an enormous and realistically tentacled squid face. My adolescent dog barely gave any of them a glance. (If you want a service dog prepared for anything, I maintain, have them raised by costumers and cosplayers.)

Last year, I brought home a fourteen-foot Velociraptor puppet. Cupcake (yes, she goes by Cupcake) is a realistic dinosaur, with blinking eyes, articulated movement, and a catalog of recorded roars, barks, grunts, and chirps. Undómiel, my adolescent Doberman, walked boldly up to this new arrival and sniffed her briefly on the nose before deciding she'd rather chew on an old bone while we worked. Penny, the above-mentioned guide candidate, did not even bother to sniff Cupcake — she simply walked up and flopped next to her, using her as shade.

It's not that Cupcake isn't a scary beast. She's startled a number of people, and while puppeteering her at a fundraising event I heard a terrified alarm bark and froze, knowing someone's service dog had just been horribly disrupted. To be fair, even the most thorough service dog training program may not prepare a dog for encounters with long-extinct enormous beasts.

But to prepare our dogs, we don't have to cover *everything*. We just have to teach them how to approach novelty. And my dogs had seen enough to adapt on the fly to even extreme novelty.

I think that a mindful and assessing approach to new situations, or as my colleague Casey Lomonaco calls it "curiosity as a life skill," can be taught, and it's hugely beneficial.

The amount of positive feedback I've received on my previous training book *Fired Up, Frantic, and Freaked Out* has just been astounding to me. People have reported great successes working with their pets, and a few confessed to "adapting" the same management techniques for use on themselves to stay calm and focused in uncomfortable situations (because good training techniques apply to all species). I couldn't be more pleased and grateful.

But as a trainer, I know we cannot be satisfied with merely fixing problems. Problem-solving is great, sure—but preventing problems is more efficient, and that should always be Plan A. We should be proactive rather than reactive. So that is where this book comes in.

Most of us know that socialization is critical in a young dog's life, both to equip them to live safely and happily in a human-centric world and to prepare them for training, whether that be for manners, a competition career, or more serious work, perhaps as a service or detection dog. While word has certainly gotten around that socialization is important, there's still a popular disconnect over what it is exactly and how best to go about it.

I used to get a lot of calls from potential clients wanting a group training class because they heard socialization was important and that seemed the best way to go about it. When I would explain that an hour-long class a week was not really going to address their socialization needs, there was a lot of confusion. Wasn't that the whole point of a puppy class?

Many of the most egregious mistakes are made by those with the best of intentions who were given bad advice. It's both heart-breaking and all too common for a trainer to be called to work with a fearful or aggressive dog and discover that the problem was inadvertently created by a well-intentioned owner trying to do the right thing but acting upon poor advice. This is unfair to both dog and owner, and it can be prevented through making good information available and accessible.

This is not a puppy training book, not in the sense of

teaching manners and basic exercises. My goal in this book is not to offer a comprehensive view of the science of socialization, but to provide a practical guide to those who want to give their dogs—whether chosen as working dogs or pets—the best start at understanding our world and how to function happily and productively in it.

There are some fantastic puppy programs now available which focus on socialization, with lots of field trips and assigned homework. While it would be ideal for every new puppy owner to have a Puppy Start Right[1] course around the corner, that's unfortunately not the case (yet!), and most of us have to work on our own. This book is intended to fill the gap where a stellar socialization program isn't readily available as a package, allowing you to create and customize your own.

Happy training!

---

[1] www.PuppyStartRight.com

Chapter 1 Socialization is important— whatever it is.

HOW COULD THIS CUTE FACE
GROW UP TO BE TROUBLE?

Socialization is important.

Ask any new puppy owner, trainer, or veterinarian, and you'll hear exactly that. Socialization is important.

But when you ask what socialization *is*, you'll get a variety of different answers.

- "Socialization is meeting different people and dogs."
- "Socialization is getting used to things."
- "Socialization is attending a puppy class."
- "Socialization is meeting kids."
- "Socialization is learning how to get along in a human world."

While none of these is technically incorrect as far as they go, they also do not offer pet owners a working definition of what socialization actually *is*. They're all paths *toward* socialization, but they are not socialization. And if we want to use socialization as a defense against a whole array of behavior problems in the future—as we should—we should probably know what it is, how to accomplish it, and the benefits we expect to derive from it.

In the human world, socialization is the adaptation and acquisition of norms, customs, and values of a society or social group. The socialization of human children includes language acquisition, cultural habits, racial egalitarianism or prejudice, and much more.

Applied to pet ownership, and for the purpose of this book, we can assume a similar definition: the acquisition of cultural habits and social communication to equip an individual to live in society.

If we want our dogs to be acceptable, happy, welcomed, and safe in human society, we need to socialize them to human social norms.

It's a deceptively simple concept, until we remember that we are working with another species entirely, and specifically one which is hardwired to sniff, dig, pull against restraint, jump up or burrow noses into private parts to greet friends, protect food and other resources, and to potentially employ sharp teeth when personal space is invaded. We are attempting to socialize a species which has no natural knowledge or understanding that that carpet is less appropriate for elimination than grass, that hugs and kisses are intended to communicate "love," or that food can be "off-limits" despite being on a perfectly-accessible table. We are addressing a species which, despite thousands of years of selective breeding, has no hardwired instincts to ignore a vacuum cleaner.

We have our work cut out for us.

Now, we do have advantages in those thousands of years of selective breeding, and we have even more in choosing our individual companions and in training. But if we want all the benefits of socialization, we need to approach it intelligently and intentionally.

What Are The Benefits?

So what are the benefits of implementing socialization protocols correctly and thoroughly?

- Reduces stimulation **threshold** and makes our subjects less excitable[2]
- Improves the learning capability of a learning-challenged subject[34]
- Enhances cognitive flexibility[5]

---

[2] Walsh RN, Cummins RA. Mechanisms mediating the production of environmentally induced brain changes. Psychol Bull. 1975;82(6):986-1000.

[3] Henderson, Norman D. Relative effects of early rearing environment and genotype on discrimination learning in house mice. Journal of Comparative and Physiological Psychology, Vol 79(2), May 1972, 243-253.

[4] Cooper, R.M. and J.P. Zubek. Effects of Enriched and Restricted Early Environments on the Learning Ability of Bright and Dull Rats. Canadian Journal of Psychology. 12(3). 1958. 159-164.

[5] Zeleznikow-johnston A, Burrows EL, Renoir T, Hannan AJ.

- Improves learning and memory in general[67]
- Increases the number of nerve endings in the brain[8]
- Reduces reactivity and unwanted "vice" behaviors in subjects genetically prone to reactivity[9]

Summing up, it makes our dogs less fearful, less reactive, and smarter. Seems like a pretty good idea, doesn't it?

What if you have adopted an older dog, who is showing the lack of socialization during the peak period? There is still some good news: effects of enrichment and behavior modification can be seen in older animals, too[10]. He may never catch up to what he might have been with proper socialization, but he can certainly improve and learn to live a more confident life.

Environmental enrichment enhances cognitive flexibility in C57BL/6 mice on a touchscreen reversal learning task. Neuropharmacology. 2017;117:219-226.

[6] Van praag H, Kempermann G, Gage FH. Neural consequences of environmental enrichment. Nat Rev Neurosci. 2000;1(3):191-8.

[7] Lazic, M., Schneider, S. M. and Lickliter, R. (2007), Enriched rearing facilitates spatial exploration in northern bobwhite (Colinus virginianus) neonates. Dev. Psychobiol., 49: 548–551.

[8] Van praag H, Kempermann G, Gage FH. Neural consequences of environmental enrichment. Nat Rev Neurosci. 2000;1(3):191-8.

[9] Grandin T. Genetics and the Behavior of Domestic Animals. San Diego : Academic Press, c1998.; 1998.

[10] "One of the most remarkable features of the enrichment studies discussed in this article is that the changes in the brain can be detected even when the enriched experience is provided to an adult or aged animal." Van praag H, Kempermann G, Gage FH. Neural consequences of environmental enrichment. Nat Rev Neurosci. 2000;1(3):191-8.

Mounting data supports the claim that training and enrichment continue to benefit the brain throughout life, both in dogs and humans[11]. We should carry on learning together for our shared maximum health. What a fun way to stay healthy!

Practical Application

I am a nerd; I love science and scientific definitions. But I have a more pragmatic definition of socialization I give my clients: **I want a dog to think rationally and proactively about any new stimulus or situation, and I want him to act intentionally and with confidence.**

In any new or confusing social situation, the dog who has learned to evaluate his options and make a rational choice is going to have an advantage. In addition, dogs who are taught to think, rather than emotionally react, are more pleasant companions.

The dog who cannot reacts to the postal worker's daily mail drop as if she were a burglar kicking in the patio door is annoying at best, and he will probably lead a less-enriched life because he will be segregated from family life more often. This dog is also significantly less useful as a home guardian, because we cannot trust his alerts and because he's more often put outside or in a back room.

---

[11] Mohammed AH, Zhu SW, Darmopil S, et al. Environmental enrichment and the brain. Prog Brain Res. 2002;138:109-33.

Likewise, the dog who never learned how to safely meet new people is going to meet fewer people, inconveniencing his owners and limiting his own life experiences. Ultimately it is for both our sake and the dog's own that we embark upon our socialization journey. It makes us all happier, more relaxed, and safer.

As a caring pet owner, you deserve a dog who thinks rationally and proactively about any new stimulus or situation, one that acts intentionally and with confidence.

Even more simply and less scientifically—every socialization encounter should end with the puppy thinking, "I win!" Whether this is gathering the courage to confidently walk past a noisy motorcycle, navigating a busy sidewalk, figuring out how to extract a treat from a puzzle toy, or working out that sitting to greet a person produces more petting than jumping, a dog who thinks through a challenge and feels confident he has met it is a dog better prepared for the *next* challenge.

A dog who feels confident and who knows how to stop and evaluate something new is a dog who will succeed in human society.

With shelters full of surrendered pets, with more young dogs euthanized for behavior problems than for disease, with breed-specific legislation presented anew in every corner, we now more than ever owe our pets a solid foundation and thorough socialization to help them live safely among us.

Lack of Socialization is Abuse

Professional trainers and veterinarians are frequently presented with dogs who are afraid of men, loud noises, quick movements, new people, reaching hands, or other innocuous but alarming events, and frequently these dogs (especially when adopted) are described as abuse survivors.

> *"The shelter people were really nice, but obviously she had been abused before she got there, because she's scared of people she doesn't know and she just hits the floor if someone comes toward her."*

On the one hand, it will probably be a relief to know that most of these dogs have not in fact been victims of physical abuse. A lack of socialization during critical stages of development in puppyhood is a primary factor in the development of these behavior challenges.

In my opinion, however, that lack of socialization can also be considered a form of abuse.

A family brought their beautiful young Labrador Retriever to group class, but he did not want to participate. He crawled through the door and then had to be half-carried to their chairs. He cowered through the class and barely ate (a sure sign of distress in a retriever!), leaving sweaty pawprints on the floor.

When I talked with them, I learned they had acquired the dog at five months old directly from the breeder—I use the term very loosely—who had kept the litter in a barn until the puppies went home. While the environment had been safe enough (the weather was fine, and the puppies probably thoroughly enjoyed wrestling through the straw and exploring the barn itself), that had been their entire world. During the prime period for socialization, when their puppy brains were categorically separating the world into normal-safe or different-dangerous, their world was limited to their mother, their siblings, one or two humans, and a single comfortable building.

Now this poor puppy was adrift in an alien world for which he had no reference, a world full of cars, leashes, dishwashers and televisions, concrete, grass, gravel, carpet, rubber matting, HVAC systems, ceiling fans, cleaner smells, cats, strange dogs, staring children, joggers, skateboards, scents of dogs who were here yesterday, and countless other obstacles we never even consider because they are so mundane to us. His family now faced months or years of conditioning him to normal life.

I consider that abuse. That puppy should never have been set up for that mental anguish. (And the family who just wanted a friendly puppy should not have been given a difficult project.)

Contrast this with a breeder who invites carefully selected strangers of varied gender, race, and age to meet the puppies, who provides them with a wide variety of novel textures and interactive substrates, who takes them on exploratory walks and introduces them to other animals and other species, who takes them on happy car rides— not just to the vet!—and makes sure they are used to all the noises of modern human society, from radio to household appliances to shrieking children, as well as introducing them to appropriate areas for elimination to keep human houses clean. This is a breeder who wants her puppies to have the best possible life, to feel comfortable in their new families and homes, to blend into human society as well as any non-human can.

This is why we socialize.

Chapter 2 Socialization Periods

TIME TO LEARN WHAT THE WORLD'S ABOUT!

W e're going to talk first about puppies. That's because socialization is primarily a puppy topic.

Yes, there are many older dogs who need to acquire these social and coping skills later in life, but technically they are not being *socialized*, because socialization is something which occurs during specific stages of development. (Some people call this process with adult dogs *familiarization*, but it does not have a technical definition. We'll talk more about adult dogs later!) The best-known socialization period is the initial period during puppyhood, lasting from 3 to 12 weeks of age.

3 Weeks Old

A puppy's sight and hearing are useful by now. He starts intentional interactions with his littermates and his mother, and he figures out the handsy bipeds who visit are a different animal altogether. He begins normalizing environments (indoors, outdoors, various surfaces underfoot) and social interactions such as learning how to get attention, learning how to acquire and defend resources (food, toys, petting, etc.), and learning how to read and respond to changes in body language and other forms of communication with his own species and others.

Singleton puppies, or puppies removed too early from the litter, are deprived of this canine socialization period and often have difficulty reading or communicating in canine body language in the future. Resist the urge to take a puppy home before 7 weeks at the earliest, and 8-10 weeks is often better.

Beware this line: "Oh, the puppies are ready to go home now, they're already weaned!"

In modern western society, most human children are weaned within their first year or two, and are they then ready to move out on their own? Of course not! Mothers are responsible for more than merely birth and lactation, and removing a puppy too early invites many problems. A breeder which offers to send a puppy home before 7 weeks is waving a red flag of warning; I would not buy from such a breeder.

7 Weeks Old

The puppy's brain is fully functional and learning is in high gear. Between 7 and 12 weeks of age, the puppy is generalizing what is "normal" in his world. Formal training can begin (using **positive reinforcement**) and our intentional socialization program should be underway.

Anything you want your puppy to accept in everyday life should be introduced during this or the previous period. If your puppy is not already accustomed from the breeder's house to household noises such as dishwashers, washing machines, televisions and background music, cars and traffic, ventilation systems, etc. then now is the time to make them normal background noise. Likewise, your dog needs to meet people of all varieties, to experience different surfaces for walking and climbing, to discover different types of weather, etc.

Remember, this is when you get to define "normal" for your puppy. It's an opportunity which won't be repeated. Do not waste this critical time for your pup.

There is some discussion whether this ideal socialization window closes at 12 weeks or 16 weeks, or if in fact it varies among breeds, sizes, or types of dogs. While that's an interesting academic discussion, our pragmatic approach remains the same: take full advantage of this critical period, starting at 8 weeks and remaining deliberate and intentional all the way through 16 weeks — because what will some extra conscientious training and socialization hurt, anyway?

8 Weeks Old

The fear impact period begins! This period from 8-10 weeks is a time when scary or painful experiences can

have a much larger and more lasting impact. Extra care should be taken to keep a puppy's experiences upbeat and confidence-building at this time.

Because this is when puppies are typically going home to new environments and families, we need to be cautious about how we handle this transfer and introduction. Make sure the puppy is introduced to people and pets with care, and let him explore the environment safely and at his own pace. More about how to do this later!

Should puppies be sequestered to prevent unpleasant experiences during this fear period? Definitely not. We're still in the primary socialization phase, and that time is not to be wasted. It does mean, however, that I will be particularly cautious about protecting my puppy from rude or inappropriate older dogs, from rude or inappropriate humans, or from unnecessary frightening or scary experiences or procedures[12].

---

[12] Note that this is the time when ear cropping is done in some breeds. Regardless of one's thoughts on whether this once-functional procedure has outlived its utility, it's undeniable that this surgery (and, in some breeds, its weeks of aftercare) takes place during a critical period.

Note that 56 days of age is a typical onset, but each dog is an individual—if you notice a fearful reaction earlier or later, don't shrug it off as "not the fear period" and ignore it. Address it using the techniques we're going to discuss.

Second Fear Period

This additional fear impact period can occur anywhere between 6 and 14 months of age and usually lasts 2-4 weeks, depending upon breed, family line, and individual dog. This is when the adolescent dog reacts oddly to things you thought were already settled, and you start to wonder if he's nuts. Don't worry, he's normal.

An example: at about 13 months old, my Doberman Shakespeare walked past a chained bicycle every day with me for three days. On the fourth day, we approached the bicycle and he lit up like it had offended him personally, hackling and showing his teeth. We worked past the bicycle and continued on our way. The next day, the bicycle offered no offense and Shakespeare ignored it as usual.

No, there wasn't a critter hiding on or behind the bicycle, and nothing else had changed—it was just his adolescent brain misfiring emotionally. Parents of human teenagers may also recognize this symptom of emotional over-reaction, perhaps? Yeah. It's a normal, if frustrating, development in adolescent brains in most species.

During adolescence the brain undergoes a "rewiring" and

integration process, often called *pruning*, in which disused neural circuits are abandoned and others are reconnected and myelinated[13] for maximum efficiency. As with any complex computer system undergoing maintenance, there may be a temporary reduction of capability and some processing mistakes. This results in what we might call, for lack of a more technical term, adolescent "brain farts."

As in the first fear period, a single bad experience during this time can set up a lifelong aversion, so be cautious. You don't need to avoid the street with the chained bicycle, but you don't want to buzz the dog with bicycles while he's worried about them.

The key to handling this second period is the same as to handling the first: avoid startling or frightening the dog, and if something does disturb him, work through it patiently, building confidence until the alarming stimulus is mundane. Please don't take any of it personally. It's normal development, and if you've laid a good foundation of socialization, it will pass.

---

[13] This is insulating the nerve cells with myelin to protect and enhance their transmission capability and speed. It makes a more efficient brain.

Chapter 3 Basics

OKAY, LET'S GET TO WORK!

While this is not specifically a training book, any time we are interacting with the dog we are training, so yes, it's a training book. As with most things, a good training foundation can make the rest of our work much simpler.

I strongly, strongly recommend using only positive reinforcement for socialization and training. Puppies are eager creatures and it is easy to reward their good behavior to encourage its repetition, and we are trying to teach them that the world is a fun place full of puzzles to be solved and games to win—from how to react to that giant noisy truck stealing our trash (hint: ignore it) to how to make a friendly new person pet you (hint: bum on ground, paws on floor). Punishing what is often exploratory behavior is contrary to our socialization goals.

This is not to say that puppies get to run amuck in our

homes. Positive, as they say, is not permissive[14]. There are definite rules and structure in a puppy's life; we can establish this structure by rewarding behaviors we like so that the puppy is likely to repeat those behaviors instead of choosing behaviors we're not so keen on.

We're not going to spend many pages going over basic training—there are many great puppy training books available, and you can find some recommended favorites in the Appendix—but there are a few absolute necessity behaviors that we need for safety and for our socialization program. Start with these training basics, and you can always add skills as you progress.

If you have an older dog rather than a young puppy, the same framework still applies. This will work for your dog, too, providing him with a solid foundation upon which you can build your training. Just substitute "dog" for "puppy" wherever appropriate in this chapter.

Targeting

I generally start with teaching the dog to "target," or make physical contact with a designated target, for several reasons:

- It's easy! Quick success builds confidence and trust in both dog and handler.
- For many dogs, it's their first introduction to

---

[14] I am not certain if Susan Garrett first coined this phrase, but she certainly popularized it.

analytical thinking—they must move their focus away from the food in the treat bag or hand, to focus on the target, to make the click happen, which produces the food they wanted.

- This analysis mirrors the assessment and thoughtful reaction we want them to practice in the real world.

I like to teach dogs to touch their nose (easy and natural) to my hand, as I'll always have it with me. I personally use two extended fingers as my target, because it doesn't look like any other gestures I'm likely to use throughout the day. (Others like to use an open hand to target the palm, or a single pointed finger, or a closed fist; whatever you choose is fine as long as you are consistent and the dog can consistently distinguish the target from other hand movements or cues.)

If your puppy is particularly short or your back is particularly stiff, you may opt to use a target stick instead of your hand. It's a good idea to teach both. This can be a commercial training product or a dowel rod with a large eraser or a wire shelving end cap on the end

Give yourself a hand

Hold the clicker in one hand, and the other will be your target. Keep your treats in your clicker hand, in a training pouch, or on a nearby table, not in your target hand; your dog most likely already comes toward food, and we don't need to train that!

Keep your clicker hand away from the dog, perhaps at your side or behind your back, both to avoid confusing him with too many options and to avoid clicking near his face or ears.

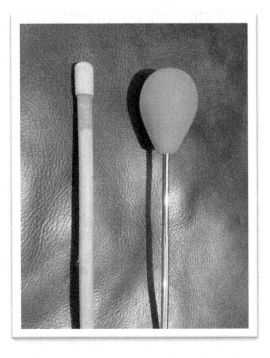

to make a safe tip. You can extend this down in front of your puppy so he can reach his target without you straining your back.

With your thumb on the clicker, present your opposite-hand target at nose-height or lower to the dog (without jabbing it at his face). Almost every dog will sniff at it interestedly—"Hey, you just stuck something out here! Is it cool?"—and that gives you a chance to click the nose moving toward the target.

Be sure your target hand is still; the dog should move to reach the target, not the other way around, and many dogs won't reach for something that's moving toward them. Also be sure to withdraw your target immediately after the click, and wait until the dog has finished chewing and swallowing before presenting it again.

If the dog licks or mouths your target, you're clicking just a bit too slowly. Try clicking sooner, even before the dog's nose reaches your target.

If the dog is grabby about the treats, simply drop one to deliver; don't try to teach two things (targeting and treat manners) at the same time. Be sure to take away your target hand after the click and then present it again after the dog has finished the treat. There should be a clear start and end to each repetition.

A typical training session should run 30-60 seconds for a puppy, and only a little longer for a novice adult dog. Resist the urge to push longer, even if you're doing well; that's a great time to stop, before any mistakes happen! When your dog really understands this behavior, you should be completing about 15 or more target repetitions per minute.

Adding a Cue

How are we doing? Assess your training session with these tests in mind:

- Your dog is watching for the target
- You can present it to the right or left and he'll touch reliably
- You can present it high or low and he'll touch reliably
- You can easily achieve 15 target repetitions in a minute

If you can meet these criteria, you're ready to add the verbal cue.

A cue is the prompt for a behavior, the "green light" to go

ahead and do a trained behavior, a limited opportunity to earn reinforcement. For pet dogs these are most often verbal (such as the word "sit") or visual (a hand signal).

My litmus test to assess whether a behavior is ready for a cue is my famous (infamous!) $50 bet—if you're willing to slap money on the table and say "Watch this! Fifty bucks says he'll nail it as soon as I put a target out there!" you're ready to attach a cue. If you're willing to bet $5, but not $50, you're not ready to use a verbal cue yet. Give it a bit more practice.

Why wait to use the cue? There are two very good reasons.

Learned irrelevance is the phenomenon of tuning out data which has no real meaning. You might notice that a dog can catch the word "walk" or "bath" but will ignore most of what you say while talking on the telephone. Dogs learn to ignore "meaningless" human noise which isn't yet attached to a clear concept, and it can be harder to retrain a snappy response to those words later.

The other reason is that we want good, reliable responses to our cues. If we teach the dog the cue in the earliest stages of the behavior, while the behavior is still uncertain and unreliable, we're associating the cue with that uncertain, unreliable behavior! By waiting until the behavior is solid, we can attach a more solid cue.

Attaching a cue to a target is simple—with your hand neutral and still, say your new cue ("Touch") and *then* present your target. Keep your hand still while you speak; he needs to hear the cue by itself and see that it predicts the hand signal he already knows and loves. (Note: this stillness may be harder than it sounds, but it matters.)

When he touches your hand target, click and treat. (If you are tempted to repeat the word, the delay means he's still having to think about the target behavior, and he's not ready for the cue yet. Practice without a verbal cue until you're ready for the $50 bet!) Repeat until you can see him looking for your hand when you say, "touch."

Advanced trainers may note that this is not full stimulus control, but it's all we need to get started on our socialization work.

Now practice randomly throughout the day, surprising your dog with "touch" at odd moments. He will be happy to do so (and he should be consistently reinforced).

If you're training in a new place, or with a distraction present, remember that $50 bet—it's perfectly acceptable to review the behavior without the verbal cue until you're certain he's ready for it! You don't want to practice associating the cue with either frustration or failure, only sweet success.

You are going to **reinforce** every time you ask for a target during socialization outings. Don't worry about fading the treats yet; it's more important to focus on socialization success and strong behaviors to support that. Fading treats is a distant second concern.

Orient to your Human

This looks like the silliest of games, but it's secretly teaching some critical skills for both dog and handler.

Toss a treat on the floor—just a freebie. Your puppy will probably dive on it or chase it, and that's fine. Let him finish it, and then *wait*. You may be tempted to call him or move or flash another treat. Wait until he finishes chewing, sniffing, licking the carpet, and looks up at you. Click that instant when he brings his head up to glance at the human.

This doesn't have to be perfect eye contact; very young or very short puppies may not even be able to find your face so quickly just yet! You are clicking just for the orientation to you.

Drop another treat after the click, so that the puppy has to break focus on you to find and eat the treat. Do not hand  the puppy the treat; we are deliberately taking his attention away from us. Why? So he can practice putting his attention on us. If we are busy holding his attention, he learns to focus only as long as we entertain or distract him. By pushing his attention away and then reinforcing his choice to refocus, we are teaching him to consciously choose to look for us and watch for signals (or treats!).

In the beginning, it may take your pup a moment to realize there's nothing else terribly interesting on the floor and to think of looking to you. (Set yourself up for success by starting this game in a boring place with nothing interesting on the floor! Bathrooms, laundry rooms, or kitchens without spilled food are good options; patches of forest with mouse trails are for advanced work!) Just be patient. It won't be long before he is snatching his tossed treat and then immediately turning back to you.

This silly game will become a great barometer for tracking your dog's mental state during your socialization field trips. If you're playing this game in a parking lot, and he feels the need to keep checking around him instead of focusing on what he knows will get him an immediate treat, it's an early indicator that he's not really comfortable in this environment—and we get insight before we ask for cued behaviors which will fail, or try to initiate a challenging encounter.

It's also good practice for the human end of the leash to stand and wait for the puppy to process his options—sniff the empty floor, or look up for another cookie—and make the most productive decision. Resist the urge to coax or cheerlead; this is about the puppy learning to refocus himself and think proactively. The future benefits are well worth the short wait now.

If you get into a situation which is just a bit much for your puppy, this is a great exercise to go back to. It's familiar, it's easy, it has guaranteed reinforcement, and it allows you to see exactly when he's comfortable again because his responses will quicken to normal rates. It's also easy to segue from this exercise into other training or socialization exercises, dropping a treat to reinforce a behavior and then using the puppy's renewed focus to give the next cue. Sweet!

Recall

This is a basic safety exercise as well as a good cue to have during socialization outings. If you have already started your hand target exercises, it's simple to turn that into a recall.

Start with a few basic hand targets to warm up, and then toss one of the earned treats a short distance away from you (on a bare floor, so it's easy to find). Watch the puppy chase the treat and eat it, and when he looks back at you, put your target hand out for him to see. He'll probably hurry back to touch it again, because he likes tasty treats and this is a 100% sure way to get one.

(Remember how we taught our puppy to eat his treat and immediately reorient to his person? That game makes this game progress more smoothly and quickly. Momentum in training!)

Click his nose touch to your hand, and throw the treat a short distance away again. As he eats the treat and lifts his head, call "Come!" As he turns to you, put your target hand out for him to come and touch.

The order of this is very important!

1. Puppy finds and eats treat
2. Handler calls "come"
3. Puppy turns to handler
4. Handler puts out target hand

If the puppy sees the target before he hears the cue "Come," he's going to focus on the visual target and the verbal cue becomes much less salient and important. If we want him to learn a response to the verbal cue—handy for when he's not already looking at us!—then we need to make sure we present the verbal cue first, before the visual cue he already knows.

Click when he reaches you and toss the treat away for him to chase, a little further this time. Repeat, adding distance gradually.

After several sessions of this game, surprise your puppy during a boring interlude with the cue, "Come!" When he orients to you, put your target hand out and click and treat when he arrives. Repeat this game, surprising him with a recall cue when he's not expecting it, until he whips around at the sound of the cue and begins running even before you can show him the visual target.

As he gets the idea of this game, you can start increasing distractions, calling him away from smells or chewing a toy or watching something interesting. Make sure you reinforce well enough that there's never a question of whether it was worth coming to you instead of staying where he was. This is where I break out the seriously tasty treats, like cheese or roast meats or hot dogs, in many tiny pieces[15]. I like to overpay recalls and build wealth in my reinforcement account, in case I ever need to make an emergency withdrawal.

It's very important when you start this training that you call him only when you know he can respond successfully. If he's new to this and is eating spilled pancakes off the floor or wrestling with another dog, don't use your recall cue—you'll only teach him that ignoring it pays very well! Remember that $50 bet, and be conservative with your gambling. You definitely don't want to teach him that this word is irrelevant. Distractions can come later, *after* he fully understands and is good at this exercise!

---

[15] The largest treat size I typically use for hand delivery is equivalent to the size of a pea.

Chapter 4 Meeting Humans

LET'S MEET SOME NEW PEOPLE.

T his is the most commonly known part of socialization—meeting people! It's no secret that introducing a puppy to strangers is part of a well-balanced program for future good behavior and safe encounters. From Dr. Ian Dunbar's suggestion of "100 people in 100 days" to "pass the puppy" exercises in group puppy classes, this is a hugely popular concept.

Unfortunately, this is one of the most misunderstood aspects of socialization, and one place where many puppy owners, while trying to do the right thing, actually set themselves up for problems later.

Let's talk about meeting humans.

Humans Don't Meet Puppies. Puppies Meet Humans.

First, I have a rule for meeting dogs with very, very few exceptions. This rule applies to puppies meeting children, to my great-aunt meeting my new dog, to me meeting client dogs—it's universal.

The human may invite the dog to meet her, but it is the dog who decides to approach the human, not the human who approaches the dog.

This very simple distinction goes far in preventing unwanted reactions to new people during the socialization process. With no need to seek an escape route—often unavailable, if the dog is on-leash or in close quarters or simply thinks he doesn't have one—and no need to be defensive of space, defensive behavior need not ever occur. This single rule for dog-human introductions could prevent thousands of bites to children and scary experiences for both species.

EARS BACK, EYES AWAY, TONGUE LICKING LIPS— THIS DOG IS GIVING EVERY POLITE INDICATION HE WANTS OUT, BUT HE IS TRAPPED. WHAT HAPPENS WHEN HE REALLY WANTS TO GET AWAY?

The process for introducing dogs and humans, whether the dog is greeting a child, an adult, or a trained professional, is the same.

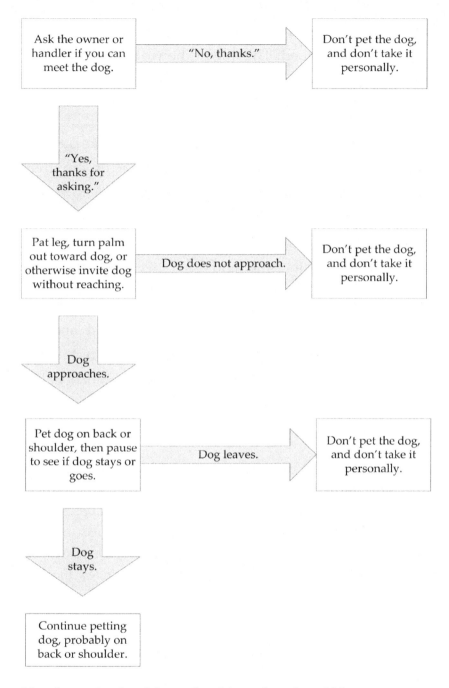

| Ask the owner or handler if you can meet the dog. | → "No, thanks." → | Don't pet the dog, and don't take it personally. |

↓ "Yes, thanks for asking."

| Pat leg, turn palm out toward dog, or otherwise invite dog without reaching. | → Dog does not approach. → | Don't pet the dog, and don't take it personally. |

↓ Dog approaches.

| Pet dog on back or shoulder, then pause to see if dog stays or goes. | → Dog leaves. → | Don't pet the dog, and don't take it personally. |

↓ Dog stays.

| Continue petting dog, probably on back or shoulder. |

Key here is the idea of asking the dog if he wants to interact with a new person, and then respecting that answer. If the dog knows he can leave at any time, he's not going to feel trapped. This means he won't feel a need to become defensive; he can simply leave any situation which makes him uncomfortable.

I find that my female clients often grasp this more quickly, due to social experience. You know that guy on the street who wants to chat you up, and when you try to ignore him, he follows you and keeps talking to you despite all social signals to leave you alone? You know how that's awkward, uncomfortable, and even creepy? Yeah, don't be that guy. Dogs don't like it either.

In *Fired Up, Frantic, and Freaked Out*, I talked about a client's dog who was aggressive to children—not *despite* her socialization experiences with dozens of children, but *because* of them. Since she never had control over her exposure, she felt overwhelmed and frightened.

> *Because she was quiet and still, and probably even exhibited some tail-wagging and licking and other please-I'm-just-a-puppy-don't-hurt-me appeasement behaviors, it may have looked like the pup was learning to like kids. As she grew older, however, she ceased the puppy appeasement behaviors and concluded that the best defense is a good offense.*

The owner had the very best of intentions, but his adult dog bit a child and he had to call for help.

Letting the puppy control the proximity and pace is key to building confidence and comfort.

Invite the dog to approach the human. As with our environmental socialization games, this allows us to accurately gauge the dog's interest and confidence.

Polite Greetings

Now that we have a way to introduce dogs and humans, let's get started.

As a general rule, we will not allow our dogs to get too physical with the people they meet, climbing them, grabbing them, holding them with legs or mouth, body-slamming them. We don't consider this polite behavior and we don't want to encourage it.

The same is true in the other direction, too. People greeting my puppy may not grab him, roll him, squeeze him, push him, or otherwise manhandle him. This can potentially frighten a shy puppy—and if you have an exuberant extrovert who loves this sort of thing, you'll probably regret teaching him that it's an acceptable way to say hello. Either way, it's best not to go there.

Dogs don't get to maul people. People don't get to maul dogs.

Now there may be a place for physical play, when a puppy is both clearly interested in engaging and has been specifically invited to get rowdy (perhaps with a particular toy reserved for rougher play). But that is a separate thing from greetings, which should be polite and civilized affairs. Do not teach your puppy that casual encounters are wild play sessions, or you will set yourself up for muddy pawprints, frustration barking and leash lunging, and a lot of remedial training.

Controlling the Situation

Often our dogs are easier to train than our fellow humans, because we have better control of the consequences for our puppies than for most of the humans in our lives. No matter how I say, "Please wait while I—" an excited stranger may dive down for my puppy and violate all my rules and precepts of socialization. When his hands hit my puppy, *boom!* instant reinforcement for his charging ahead despite my pleas. And in the meantime, my puppy may be learning the world is not as safe as he thought, and he might be thinking of how to get away.

I need a backup plan.

Remember that target training we practiced? This is another great place to use it. If I see my puppy getting pounced, I can call him to target my hand (which will coincidentally happen to be just out of reach of the grasping children or excited stranger or whoever). I can then reinforce the targeting or, if necessary, collect the puppy and pick him up out of harm's way.

This works even if the puppy is off-leash—and if he's on-leash, it will still be my first choice. Tightening the leash to pull him backward will make him feel more trapped (tight leash means fewer places to go), and being dragged backward is not exactly a fun experience even if he's not already worried about whatever is going on. Getting him to remove himself also teaches him to walk away from an uncomfortable social situation as a first option rather than getting defensive, an important skill I'll want him to have as an adolescent and adult.

What if our target or recall training isn't ready yet for this level of distraction, or if my puppy freezes instead of runs back to me? Get in there and help him! Feel no hesitation in picking up a puppy or stepping in front of a dog who did not want to meet a person. You are under no obligation to let anyone handle your dog, even if they "really like dogs," and especially not if they did not ask you or heed your directions. Don't feel bad about stepping in for your puppy's benefit. If you've ever wanted rescued at a party or date gone bad, you know how your dog feels at this moment. Be his hero.

Breed & Personality Variations

A friend knelt to meet baby Laevatein, who was about ten weeks old. Laev looked at him, sniffed him, gave an almost visible shrug, and went back to playing with a more fascinating twig on the ground. "Wow," he said, "you'd better get on that."

He meant that a puppy who was standoffish at ten weeks was likely to show some social issues later in life, and I needed to step up my socialization with her.

He wasn't wrong—a puppy who shows no interest in meeting people may have a serious problem. This is a species we've selectively bred for thousands of years to like us and bond with us, and the trusting infants should reflect that heritage.

But some dogs are bred to be more inherently social than others, and Laevatein was a working-lines Doberman, a breed which is described as "aloof" in the breed standard. She'd met a lot of people already, and she just didn't care about this guy at this moment. That was normal for her temperament. Indeed for the rest of her life, Laevatein often enjoyed meeting people (she even certified as a therapy dog and clearly liked her limited experience there), but it was always a casual thing for her. People were nice and all, but she came to *work*.

My dog Penny, on the other hand, is a Labrador Retriever, and specifically a Labrador Retriever bred for service dog work. She *adores* meeting new people, and any sign of hesitation or disinterest from her would be a major warning signal to me that something was wrong and needed immediate attention.

My friend was used to a more gregarious breed temperament, and so Laevatein's disinterest to him looked like reticence or shyness. Both of those would be signs of socialization problems! Occasional disinterest, however, is a normal part of the Doberman temperament.

Keep in mind that consistent disinterest, however, is more likely to be misinterpreted anxiety. Again, puppies normally should be outgoing and curious. It's perfectly normal for a puppy to meet a person and then wander away sometimes. A puppy who consistently hangs back or engages in other behaviors may be finding something else to do so he doesn't have to interact with the stranger, and that's where I do have to kick up my socialization game.

Facilitating Introductions

If a puppy doesn't feel comfortable approaching a new person, it's time to use that handy target again.

One often hears the advice to have the stranger feed some treats. While this isn't always a bad idea and can work well for a hesitant dog, for a truly worried puppy it may be too much. I call it the "candy from strangers" approach. *Why should I take food from you? And it's scary being this close to you anyway!*

Have the new person put out a hand target exactly like you present yours, preferably low to the ground but without bending forward over the puppy's approach path. (If he needs to get lower, have him squat or turn sideways so that he's not leaning toward the puppy, which can create a very intimidating picture from near the ground.) He may need to look away, and I usually suggest he should watch my face instead of the puppy.

Let the puppy build his courage to work toward and then finally reach toward the hand target. It's okay if he doesn't quite touch it—click him as he's working up to it! And then treat him back near you, not over by the new person.

This reinforces the puppy for approaching the scary new person, without trying to keep him too close for comfort. It also sets him up to approach from a safe distance again the next time.

After he finishes his treat, release him to approach and touch the stranger-target again. Again, click and treat his effort. If he's looking more confident, click the next time, but have the new person drop the treat on the ground instead of you delivering the treat. Build up, at the puppy's own pace, to the puppy taking the treat from the stranger after his click.

Most puppies work through this progression in a minute or so. If your puppy takes longer to feel comfortable, with several different people, it might be good to consult a professional trainer (see the Appendix) in case your puppy needs a more intensive approach than is defined within this book. It's much easier to address these issues earlier than later.

Chapter 5 Meeting Others

I THINK THIS IS THE BEGINNING
OF A BEAUTIFUL FRIENDSHIP.

One common misconception about socialization is that it is about meeting people and dogs. In fact, it's about meeting *everything*.

If we introduce a young dog only to dogs and stationary adult humans, he's going to be fairly boggled when he meets a cat—or a pet snake, or a skateboarder, or even a dog with an unusual visual aesthetic (I'm looking at you, Poodle with a Continental clip). I've met some docked Dobermans who were fascinated by the fact that my natural Doberman had a full tail and couldn't take their eyes off it.

If we however introduce a young dog to cats, horses, and people in outlandish costumes or on unusual methods of locomotion (and remember, to a novice puppy, all locomotion which isn't feet is unusual), then they learn that variety exists, and they are less surprised in the future even by something they have never seen before (such as racers in running tutus).

The key, as always, is to keep the introductions light and fun. Do not force a puppy to meet anyone he doesn't want to, and make sure to end the session well before he gets tired or overwhelmed. It's quite easy for a puppy to be having a good time right up until he isn't, so err on the side of conservative when you're deciding when to quit. At the risk of cliché, always quit while you're ahead and always leave 'em wanting more. **You can go back for another successful session far more easily than you can erase a bad memory.**

> *If the puppy does not leave feeling more confident and happy than when he came, he did not have a good socialization experience.*

Always be open to unexpected opportunities, available if you keep an eye open and travel prepared[16]. I took a young Undómiel to an open air film one night, thinking we would have a relatively ordinary outing with a few dozen

---

[16] I keep a clicker and treats on hand anytime I go out with a young dog, just in case of a perfect training opportunity or a need for emergency recovery or situation management. It's never a problem to have extra treats I didn't need.

people and a new environment. I didn't realize there would be a falconer there, who could assure me that his birds hunted regularly with dogs and so would be comfortable with my puppy getting close. You never know what you might find to further expand your puppy's experiences!

Leash Guidelines

A tight leash is uncomfortable, limits mobility and can thus induce a sense of feeling trapped, and transmits owner anxiety (which is usually why the leash is tight) to the puppy. None of these are appropriate for a friendly introduction and socialization encounter. Make sure that you keep the leash loose during greetings.

This does not mean the dog gets to race directly to the friendly stranger he'll be meeting today! This is very rude and potentially very dangerous behavior. Use your hand target or treats to help him approach at a reasonable pace without hauling on the leash or charging his new friend.

Bailing Out

As challenging as it can be to teach fellow humans how best to meet our impressionable young puppy, it gets more complicated when we bring in other species or objects, because we can't explain what we're doing and ask for cooperation. Other dogs may be very interested in your pup and don't care if you're concerned the encounter may be going too fast, and a typical cat or horse isn't going to stand quietly and wait until you give permission to say hello.

This means it is critical that you have a way to draw your pup out of an encounter if necessary. Again, this is where I rely heavily on the nose targeting we practiced earlier. A quick nose target is not only a great way to keep an excited puppy focused on you (and thus not rushing rudely to another dog or other animal, who might not take it well), it's a fast way to bring him away from a situation which is going south, letting you lead him as far away as is necessary in one smooth motion, even while your eyes might be focused back where you were.

And again, pulling him back by the leash is not going to be Plan A in case the need should arise for a judicious retreat. Just as we discussed before, tightening the leash gives the puppy fewer options and makes him feel trapped, even before we add the disorienting and potentially physically painful jerk backwards. It sets up a timeline for a lesson we don't want to teach:

This might well lead him to the conclusion that he should prevent the discomfort by interrupting the process:

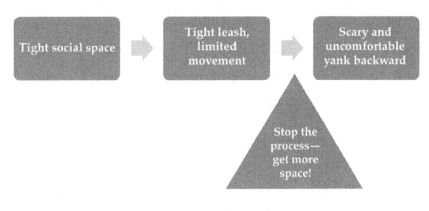

Or perhaps he should disrupt the flow toward trouble even earlier:

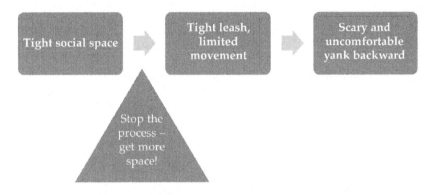

In his mind, snarking at someone or something who is too close is a perfectly logical response, because tight social situations create discomfort and he needs to move them away in order to protect himself. In this way, we can accidentally create a dog with social anxieties during well-meaning attempts to socialize him.

If we call or target him out of a sketchy situation, however, he not only retains full autonomy of his own body and actions (always more confidence-building than having that self-control taken away), but he practices disengaging from an uncomfortable social situation, learning that retreat is a valid menu option should he feel uncomfortable. He doesn't have to move *them* by scaring them away, he can move *himself*. And this is a critical skill.

If your dog is too intent to hear you calling him back, either you haven't done enough practice yet or he's feeling a bit overwhelmed and cannot process the additional stimulus of your cue, or he hears you but doesn't feel comfortable taking his eyes off the very close stranger. In this case, put your target hand right beside his face so that he can easily see and reach it, click and treat his first attempt[17], and then continue to lead him around and away, clicking and treating his targeting as you go.

In an emergency—say, if the other dog is giving clear warnings and may snap or bite—get the puppy out of there, even by leash if necessary. But be aware that you're making a big withdrawal on the bank account of trust you've been building, and it's going to take a lot of deposits to make up the difference.

Real-Time Walk-Through of a Greeting

So, I've chosen a dog to meet my puppy Buster. Trooper is a somewhat older dog, friendly but not too excited about

---

[17] If you've chosen a well-trained dog for him to meet, the other dog can be targeting away with her own handler at the same time, making it easier for your pup to move away as she is not fixated on him and reducing any competition for targets or treats.

other dogs, so she's likely to be social but not overwhelming or pushy.

Buster and Trooper are both on-leash for this initial encounter. As our two teams approach, I use my hand target we've practiced (clicking and treating each time) to keep Buster near me and working even though we're getting closer to Trooper. Trooper's handler is also cuing basic behaviors and treating Trooper, so if Buster ignores my cues and tries to engage her, she will ignore him and continue working for tasty treats. Buster realizes that it's to his best advantage to hang out with me and listen to my cues.

If Buster gets too excited and tries to rush Trooper, I just step back and call him to come to me and target again. My clicks and treats are fast and fluent (because we've practiced a lot!), so I'm not dropping treats or taking so long that Buster gets bored and distracted and turns back to Trooper.

When the two dogs are close and on loose leashes, I tell Buster to "say hello" and gesture him toward Trooper. He may pause and look at her for a moment, testing the waters, or he may go right up to her. I keep the leash loose and out of the way as the two dogs sniff. (Hopefully Buster had the manners to approach politely rather than rushing Trooper's face. If not, I'll make sure that the next approach brings them together at a different angle, not head-on.)

I'll give Buster and Trooper about five to ten seconds to sniff and greet. Trooper's handler and I will nod to each other to coordinate. Then I'll take a step backward (keeping the leash loose, just using my body language to help draw Buster to me) and call with either my recall or targeting cue. When Buster turns and comes toward me, leaving Trooper behind, I'll click and gush praises and treat him lavishly. That was a big challenge, and he did great!

If Buster didn't whip around to respond to my cue, that's okay—Trooper did for her human's call, so now Buster is feeling kind of lonely as his new friend leaves him to get some sweet treats. I'll keep the leash neutral, neither following him if he pulls nor pulling him to me, and I'll call him again, until he remembers that he's heard this cue before. I will click and treat this response, and I'll make a mental note that we need to practice with more distractions.

After a couple of treats, if everything continues well, I'll send Buster back to meet Trooper once more. Another few seconds, another call back. If Buster starts to look too excited or too worried, we'll take a little walk away and circle back. When we've had a friendly greeting, or before Trooper appears to be getting tired of the game, we'll walk away and do some targets for treats, so leaving is just as fun as arriving.

And Now, Not Greeting

This is an aspect of socialization which is often misunderstood or overlooked, so let me say it clearly here: **It is just as important to practice not greeting other people and dogs as it is to practice greeting.**

"But I thought socialization was all about meeting people and dogs!"

No, socialization is about recognizing normal environments and situations. The routines and behaviors our puppy practices now are the routines and behaviors he'll expect for the rest of his life. Just as teaching a tiny puppy to jump up for petting can come back to haunt you when he's a full-sized dog or covered with mud, inadvertently teaching a dog that he will always approach and play with strangers can lead to unwanted and even asocial behavior.

A dog who is taught, through consistency and repetition, that new humans and dogs always predict social hour and playtime can be a very annoying dog, indeed. You've probably known such a dog, one who could simply not settle down until he'd met the stranger, or one who barked and dragged or lunged on-leash at the sight of a new arrival, perhaps even sounding agitated or fierce while the owner assured you, "He just wants to say hi, he calms down as soon as he meets you."

Let me translate this behavior into a human equivalent.

Imagine that you walk into a party and begin a conversation with a friend. As you're mid-sentence, another attendee across the room demands, "Hey, get over here and say hello, right now! Come talk with me! I'm the one you should be here for, and I'm just gonna keep shouting at you until you give up and get over here!"

Not exactly a charming approach, is it? That behavior doesn't fly well in the human social world, either. Just as this demanding behavior can easily flow into aggression[18] in the human example, it can in the dog world as well[19].

For this reason, I practice with my puppy ignoring people and dogs at least as often as I practice greeting them. This can sound very odd at first, especially when we're talking about socialization outings, but I remind my clients that I personally spend a lot of time in public places without stopping to shake hands or hug every single person I pass.

---

[18] Frustration aggression is aggression which surfaces when the subject is denied something he wants. This is evident everywhere from kicking a stuck vending machine to throwing a video game controller after failing a level. If you'll forgive a somewhat political example, I often use the analogy for my female clients of walking alone and hearing from a catcaller first, "Hey, gimme a smile, girl!" and if they do not immediately comply, "What, you think you're too good for me, bitch?" The escalated aggression is not a reaction to any kind of threat—neither the vending machine nor the pedestrian interacted in any meaningful way with the aggressor—but is purely a venting of frustration at being denied reinforcement.

[19] Aggression is a risk in both in the obnoxious demanding dog, via frustration, and in the intended target dog, who may quite reasonably resent this rude behavior.

This not only makes my life much more efficient, but makes me more socially acceptable! (Imagine someone who had to stop and hug every person she passed in a mall, grocery, statehouse, or sidewalk. Wouldn't that be annoying, and just a little creepy?) It doesn't make me any less social or civilized to ignore people at times; it just means I recognize when it's appropriate to greet someone and when it's not.

Real-Time Walk-Through of Not-Greeting

Buster and I warm up with a few nose targets for clicks and treats, so that we're in the zone, and then we start forward on our walk. Trooper and her handler are heading our direction, too—not directly at us, which is very engaging and probably too difficult yet for Buster, but at an oblique angle, so that Buster can see Trooper perfectly well but they're not making head-on eye contact. To start, I'll have the dogs about twenty feet apart, or more if either is struggling to offer or maintain focus.

Trooper's handler is using many targets and treats[20] to keep her engaged as they walk, so she is not sending any

---

[20] If Trooper herself is not trained well enough yet to target instead of looking at the nearby puppy, a stream of high-value treats can usually bridge the gap. Treat fast enough that she doesn't have time to bother about the puppy between snacks. If Trooper cannot ignore the puppy for high-value treats, she's probably not a good candidate for this exercise. If she's really excited and unable to calm herself in the presence of other dogs, she might ask you to pick up a copy of *Fired Up, Frantic, and Freaked Out.*

indications to Buster that she's interested in him—she's too interested in her own affairs!

As we walk, I let Buster glimpse Trooper, and I ask him for a hand target. Note, I am *not* offering him a treat—I am asking him for a behavior. My goal here is not to distract him from another dog, but to ask him to focus on me and think about his own behaviors in the presence of another dog. That's a big difference.

If Buster cannot target my hand, I'm going to look at his overall body language. Is he completely wrapped around the axle mentally, unable to hear me or respond because he's so fixated on Trooper? That's exactly the response we're trying to avoid installing! I need to get out and start over before I create a bigger problem.

I will put my target right near Buster's face, or perhaps even use treats to lure him away, or if he's really mentally checked out, I may even pick him up or use the leash to (gently) bring him away to a distance where he can focus on me again. Then I'll rethink our scenario—was Trooper too close? Too head-on to Buster? Not focused on her own handler but interacting with Buster?—and try again with a better environment to ensure success[21].

If, on the other hand, he's looking at Trooper but is not lunging, barking, or otherwise losing his mind, and if Trooper is doing a good job of focusing on her own handler and ignoring Buster, I'm just going to wait. Let Buster watch a moment, maybe even give a bark or two in hopes that she'll drop the free cheese and rush to join him (not likely, if we're doing our jobs right!), and then finally get bored with the lack of interaction and turn back to me. And guess what, I just happen to have a target and clicker waiting, so that turning back to me and ignoring the other dog was *so much* more fun and useful than staring futilely over there!

I'll do a few more targets and treats, and then I'll circle away, take a short break (30-60 seconds) and then set up the same scenario again, until Buster has no hesitation in looking away from that other dog and responding to a cue.

Notice that I'm not calling or prompting Buster, but I'm letting him look around and make his own decision. I am not prompting or "helping" Buster to remember me, and I am not trying to distract him from the other dog. This is key! My goal is not to carry the responsibility of distracting Buster for the rest of his life! My goal is that he

---

[21] It's important to ensure success. No one can know what works until it works, and failing only tells a puppy (or a human) what doesn't work. Positive reinforcement is very powerful stuff, but we need something to reinforce!

learns to check out his environment, evaluate a situation, and make an educated decision about how to respond. *That* is a socialized dog. That's what I want.

I'll set up future scenarios with a bit more challenge for Buster, perhaps with Trooper angling a bit more toward us as we walk, perhaps with Trooper jogging. Eventually we'll work up to Trooper or another dog watching Buster and even barking or play-bowing at him. But the criteria for Buster is the same—ignore that other dog and respond to a cue from me, and I'll pay you better than that other dog does. If ever he can't make the right decision, I'll back up to an easier challenge and review until he can.

Note that this is easiest for Buster if we keep our cues clear. If he has to guess whether this is a meeting situation or not, sometimes he's going to guess wrong. I use "say hello" if I want my dog to greet another dog or human, and the default if I haven't given that cue is that we're not here to meet anyone. Feel free to work out whatever system you like, as long as it's consistent and clear for your dog to understand.

Remember, my goal is not to have a dog I can distract away from something in the environment, but to have a dog who can think for himself when something new or distracting is in the environment. Take the time to let your dog think through his options and show you what he can choose. It's worth it.

Level Up

Sometimes we need a dog to *really* resist distractions. Any service dog trainer will tell you that despite the explanatory vests and signs, some members of the public still feel entitled to speak to, call away, pet, or even grab working dogs[22]. To prevent the puppy from unwanted learning experiences when encountering these individuals, it's best to train the dogs in advance.

One measure I took was to teach that each time someone called, "Hey, puppy!" I would dispense cheese, one of the highest-value reinforcers in our menu. "Hey, puppy!" from a stranger became a cue to focus very hard on the handler. If they called repeatedly, trying to distract the dog (whether

Turning a distraction into a cue

To start, each time someone called "Hey, puppy!" I immediately started feeding cheese, even if the puppy looked at the distracting person. I started with a friend, who could tone down the call if it proved stronger than cheese. (It usually didn't.)

Then I started hesitating just slightly, waiting to see if, upon hearing the distracting call, the puppy would look at the caller or at me. Often they did both. "What was that? Oh, wait, that means cheese!" And I would reinforce turning back to me.

Soon puppies learned to turn straight to me for maximum cheese efficiency!

---

[22] One woman said to me, as she darted over to straddle and hug my perplexed puppy, "I know I'm not supposed to touch them but I just can't help myself."

through malice or simple entitled single-mindedness), it was just repeating the cue, inadvertently encouraging more and more focus on the handler[23] — who was of course reinforcing this good decision!

This could be generalized to a number of distracting scenarios, such as clapping hands or extending food to the service dog in training, all of which now became cues to focus on the handler instead of going to the distraction[24].

You may not need your dog to ignore all other distractions so reliably as a service dog working in public, but learning to walk past distractions and to view them instead as opportunities for reinforcement is always a good idea.

Making sure your dog has the social ability to both "say hello" and to ignore others as appropriate is a huge asset in his repertoire of social skills.

---

[23] Bonus: each time the obnoxious stranger called, "Hey, puppy!" the dog looked away, providing no reinforcement at all to the human for the unwanted behavior.

[24] It's important to note that these dogs *do* have rich social lives and do meet many people—just not while they are working.

Chapter 6 Building Confidence

"CLIMB EVERY MOUNTAIN...!"

One of the primary goals in socializing our dogs is creating confidence. A confident dog has less need to be defensive, reducing the risk of aggressive behavior. A confident dog can go more places without needing coaxing or management. A confident dog is much easier to work with at the vet clinic or grooming salon.

We've made a good start on building confidence by introducing clicker training. This kind of **operant conditioning** is all about making choices to produce a desired result[25], controlling one's own environment and experiences, and any behavior professional for any species will tell you that a sense of control is critical to confidence and mental health.

---

[25] Other forms of positive reinforcement training, such as luring into position and then treating, are still humane and dog-friendly, but they often teach a dog to wait for prompting or help if he gets stuck rather than making his own evaluations and decisions.

There are more games and exercises we can do to continue to build confidence in our young dog.

Exploration

Exploring is one of the most natural and important means of building confidence. In the wild, young canids like wolf, coyote, or fox pups are born in a protected space and then gradually venture outside, exploring at their own pace and always returning to safety if they are frightened, overwhelmed, or tired.

These pups naturally explore at their own pace and from a secure "base" to which they always know how to return, since they walked away from it only a short time before.

A mistake we often make with very young puppies, however, is taking them to a new place and setting them down with no reference point to a safe base. It's not uncommon to see a puppy freeze when first put down in a new environment, because he doesn't know where he is, which way to go, and which way to retreat if necessary.

I like to create a safe base of operations if we go on an exploratory venture, and this will be the first place the puppy is set down. This might be a crate, or a car, or my lap, or whatever is portable and secure in the puppy's mind[26]. From here the puppy can look around until he's

---

[26] A very portable version of a safe zone is training a relaxed settle on a towel or mat, which I call only half-jokingly a security blanket for

ready to explore—this might be seconds or minutes, depending on the puppy and the environment—and then he can launch on his new mission (on-leash or off-leash, depending on the environment). When he wants to retreat, he knows the way.

Older puppies are usually content to use their human as a mobile base. If we go exploring in the woods, we can go much further, because their secure base is traveling with them. (This is also called "Mom" in the natural world!) Here I will reinforce checking in with me but also encourage some independent exploration. "No worries, I'll be here when you get back."

This exploration should be fun and reinforcing for the puppy. In many cases, such as walking in the woods, the environment takes care of that itself. *So many new smells! A stick to taste! Wow, squirrel poop!*

If the environment is less inherently reinforcing, however, such as a veterinary clinic's examination room, I may need to seed the area with strategically-placed reinforcement for the puppy to discover. *Wow, someone left a piece of hot dog behind this desk! And hey, I didn't know that squeaky mice could be found in stinky vet rooms!*

---

dogs. I go into this training in detail, and ways to use it on the road, in *Fired Up, Frantic, and Freaked Out.*

Separation

It's important to let some of this exploring take the puppy away from you. In today's world of helicopter parenting and constant supervision, letting puppies play alone and without close supervision seems irresponsible. But letting a puppy build confidence and independence in this way may help to prevent separation anxiety in the future, just as in human children[27].

Let the puppy wander away from you (in safe environments, of course, such as a fenced field—not alongside a busy highway) and explore, returning on his own time or occasionally in response to a practice recall. If you don't have a large fenced area to explore, a lightweight long line can be useful.

At home, set up planned separations—crating with a stuffed puzzle toy is an easy way to set this up—and teach the puppy that it is fun to be away from you, too.

It's important to do these separations away from home as well, letting the puppy explore a friend's yard away as you sit on the deck, or crating in another room of a friend's house with a special chew. This will help to prevent separation anxiety at home and away.

[27] Sandseter EB, Kennair LE. Children's risky play from an evolutionary perspective: the anti-phobic effects of thrilling experiences. Evol Psychol. 2011;9(2):257-84.

Climbing

Part of exploring is exploring one's physical capabilities as well. Climbing in, on, over, and under are all natural exploration techniques which are important to engage, even if we don't want them practiced on the kitchen table.

You can build a playground for your pup out of boxes, stools, boards, balls, and pretty much any junk you have lying around the garage. You want to be careful that nothing can shift in such a way to pinch or crush a puppy's paws, and you want to make sure that nothing tall is so wobbly as to make a puppy fall. However, I personally like a little wobble in my puppy's play area, as I feel it develops confidence (if they can control the wobble) and proprioception or body awareness.

I don't really worry about building something too challenging. By letting the puppy set his own pace, he will go only as fast and far as he feels comfortable. Left to their own choice, most puppies tend to push themselves to their current limits, and go further only as they feel more capable.

There is a great psychological benefit to exploring or trying something which feels very risky, and navigating it on one's

own. This is an important part of physical, social, and emotional development.[28]

This seems to be true with human children as well. Statistics show more frequent and more severe injuries per person on our modern standardized and "safe" playgrounds than on older, more varied equipment without rubber matting and well-padded mulch to absorb the shock of ground impact—probably because children who perceive less risk are less careful and thus more likely to be injured.

I'm not advocating a completely reckless approach; the physical considerations mentioned in Chapter 8 are important. But we should not be so concerned about a low risk of stunting a puppy physically that we run a high risk of stunting him mentally.

I also let my puppies climb on a FitPAWS® Donut, first braced for just a hint of instability, gradually more and more wobbly, and eventually completely unsupported so that they must balance it themselves. We practice position changes[29] on this surface so they can learn body control and focus despite distractions and challenges. Typically this rapidly becomes a favorite game and they are terribly

---

[28] Sandseter EB, Kennair LE. Children's risky play from an evolutionary perspective: the anti-phobic effects of thrilling experiences. Evol Psychol. 2011;9(2):257-84.
[29] Sit, down, and stand, all cued on the unstable surface and not lured or physically prompted, both of which can disrupt a puppy's balance.

disappointed when they outgrow the donut! While this isn't necessary for all dogs, dogs intended for working careers or physically challenging sports can benefit from this extra body awareness and surface confidence.

Make sure your puppy experiences natural and manmade, textured and slippery surfaces. Remember that as with most conditioning, it's not about exposing to all possible variations so much as it is about introducing the concept of variation, so that novelty is not a surprise.

Touch the Goblin

This phrase is borrowed from Alexandra Kurland, whose work with horses—a large prey animal whose natural instinct when sensing threat is high-speed flight—requires careful socialization and conditioning to novelty.

Alex, like many trainers of all species, asks her horses to nose-target the thing which is new or frightening. Much like the "Look at That" game popularized and named by Leslie McDevitt, this serves multiple purposes all at once:

- The animal has a specific behavior to focus on
- This behavior has a strong history of reinforcement, invoking emotional pleasure
- The scary thing becomes a target itself, a source of potential reinforcement, **counter-conditioning** the scary thing and reducing its power as a source of potential alarm

This request to "touch the goblin" can be scaled up or down as the dog requires in that situation.

First, simply give the dog a moment to assess the situation. A child who comments, "It's raining," and gets the response, "Oh, it's nothing to worry about! We have candles in case the power goes out and plenty of food and we can go upstairs in case of flooding!" is going to have a very different picture of weather than the child who comments, "It's raining," and hears in response, "Yes, looks like it."

Let the dog decide if he's really worried or not. Sometimes, after a few seconds of observation, he realizes that the scary thing really isn't so scary after all.

If he decides that he's not worried and goes back to chewing on his toy or doing something else unconcerned, let him. If he decides that he's not worried and goes to investigate, praise him for his boldness.

If however he decides that he probably is worried after all, you may want to ask him to touch the goblin. Place your hand between him and the scary thing, much closer to him than the goblin, and cue a nose target. Click when he touches your hand.

Now, the important part—deliver the treat to the side, *away* from the scary thing. Resist the urge to use the treat to lure him closer. Resist, I say! It is tempting, but that only shows us the power of the lure, not the dog's view of the situation. A treat can temporarily distract a dog, especially a young puppy, from his situation, but when it's gone, he's suddenly confronted with it almost as an unpleasant surprise. ("Hm, tasty, and—ohmygosh that's close!") In addition, I've seen many dogs lured into an uncomfortable situation who then suddenly decide they can't take any more and either snap or bolt, neither of which we want happening here.

Placing the treat a little bit away from the scary thing, so that dog is further from it than where he started, sets us up to use the target to ask him to return. Since he was already there before, it's an easy request and an easy win. Move him away with the treat delivery and repeat, this time a tiny bit closer. The momentum of his behavior in going and returning will carry him better than one long stretch of trying to edge him closer.

The movement also provides some stress relief, both physically and mentally (disengaging and then reengaging with the scary thing). While feeding for a prolonged time close to the scary thing might seem helpful, there is no relief and stress will build, making it a bigger challenge than approaching and immediately leaving.

You may or may not work the puppy all the way up to the scary thing. That's okay. The important part is that he learned he could think and earn treats even while the scary thing was in his environment, and he was still in control of his actions and able to make choices. If he were picked up and taken near the scary thing, he might have eventually discovered it wasn't as scary as he thought, but he would have learned nothing about how to cope with something new and alarming. (He also might justly infer that when something scary appears, his options are removed.)

Remember, socialization is not just about exposure, it's about learning what to do in future exposure.

Touch the Goblin Walk-Through

Let's say my puppy Buster and I are walking through a parking lot when a motorcycle pulls in to park near us. Buster is alarmed by this noisy, stinky thing which has just zoomed unexpectedly past, and after a few moments he is still giving it the side-eye, so I see we need to touch the goblin.

I ask the owner of the motorcycle to stay still as we approach, just keep texting on his phone like he's been doing since he parked. (Most of the time I find people are very willing to work with you for the sake of a startled puppy.) I don't want him reaching for Buster or doing anything to add complexity to our situation. Buster only needs to think about the bike and his target.

I put my target just in front of Buster's nose as he watches the motorcycle. He's happy to have a favorite behavior to think about instead of the weird bike, so he immediately touches my hand, and I deliver his treat about a foot back from where he's standing. Then I present my hand target again, asking him to return to where he was looking at the bike.

This is pretty simple, since it's right where he just was, so he goes back for another click and treat. I reset him a foot back again, and then this time I ask for an extra few inches to reach my target. He hesitates, but complies, and I reset him a short distance back.

I ask for a few inches more this time, only about a foot away from the motorcycle itself, and Buster decides that's too close, clearly within puppy-eating range. He holds his distance. I withdraw my hand target, count three seconds, and then extend it again, but this time on a path parallel with the bike, to the side of Buster. He has to take a few steps to reach the target, but none of them are closer to the bike, so after a moment of consideration he does. I reset him nearer me with the treat, and the next time he is

willing to take a step nearer the bike itself.

I think I could use the target to bring him all the way to the bike, but I don't want to risk him touching it and getting his nose burned, ending on a bad experience, so I decide to quit while we're ahead. He doesn't need to physically touch it today; he's already conquered his fear of it by working so well beside it and focusing on the target instead of the motorcycle. I use the last target to lead him away from the bike and treat him. And then I might ask if he and the biker would like to meet, if Buster enjoys meeting new friends and they are both up to that.

Make sure you always reset the dog away from the scary thing between repetitions, setting him up to turn back to face and walk toward the object again. Remember, the goal is not to get the dog *close* to the scary thing—the goal is to get the dog *to approach* the scary thing. It's a subtle distinction, but important.

Chapter 7 Field Trip!

*I' M READY—
LET' S HIT THE ROAD!*

P lanned socialization outings are critical for most of us, as there is just not enough in our homes to count as encounters. In fact, I tell clients that anything at home doesn't count at all for public socialization—even if you have other dogs and people at home, for example, that's nothing like meeting dogs and people in public. To put it in human terms, there are plenty of humans who have siblings but are still rude or socially awkward.

We have to go out and actively seek out places to visit and things to experience with our young dogs.

Vaccinations

Fortunately, the old-fashioned advice to keep a puppy indoors or at home until he has finished his complete series of puppy vaccinations is being replaced with more puppy-friendly recommendations, which allow pet owners to socialize their puppies strategically while protecting their developing immune systems.

Consider a human infant. When we bring her home from the hospital, do we then bar the door and keep her from seeing the outside world until her early vaccinations are complete at six years old? No, that would be ridiculous. We pack her up and take her to the grocery, to the park, to show off at Grandma's. A child who never saw human society until she was six would be severely socially stunted.

The same is true for puppies. Keeping them at home during the most critical socialization period is negligent at best. The veterinary industry, even while chiefly concerned with puppy vaccinations and risk of disease[30], agrees that socialization is too important to postpone[31].

Now, we should still take sensible precautions with both human and canine infants. I probably won't let either play on the floor of their respective hospitals, for example, where sick patients have been vomiting or shedding virus or creating other high-risk exposure. I won't take an unvaccinated puppy to a dog park and he won't touch the floor in high-traffic pet areas, such as pet supply stores.

---

[30] This is not in any way intended to denigrate the veterinary industry, but their primary concern has traditionally been physical health, not behavior. That was behind the early recommendation to keep puppies home until their vaccinations were finished. More and more vets today are adopting the idea that behavioral health is an equally important component of overall health and patient welfare.

[31] You can find the ASVAB statement on early socialization at http://bit.ly/2mtvfmV.

But I am absolutely going to take him on socialization outings. It's far too risky not to.

Gear

Let's talk for a moment about safety equipment.

Leash

A leash is not so much a joystick for steering the dog, but rather a safety line for if something goes wrong. I usually use a four- or six-foot leash for typical outings, which provides plenty of space for moving toward and away from friendly strangers or scary objects without offering too much opportunity for tangling. A lightweight long line can be useful for longer-range exploration, such as in an unfenced field.

I am not a fan of retractable leashes for many reasons, but especially not for puppies and socialization outings. The spring-loaded mechanism keeps a constant pressure on the dog, undermining everything we've discussed thus far about the importance of a loose leash. If a dog circles while meeting another person or dog, they are much more difficult to untangle on the fly. In addition, anyone who has ever gotten a retractable leash injury can attest it is exactly the opposite of a positive experience[32]. Invest in a comfortable four- or six-foot leash and use it for the next decade or more.

---

[32] Search Google images at your own risk.

Collar

Our dogs are always wearing flat, buckle collars[33] or properly fitted body harnesses for socialization outings, no choke chains or pinch collars. I want something safe, secure, and unlikely to give any unintentional discomfort at a key moment.

Treat Pouch

And I always carry treats, just in case. If we don't need them, no harm done. But if we encounter something scary or I happen upon the perfect training scenario, I'll be glad I have them. A belted treat pouch (mine has a wide, magnetic-closure mouth) takes about a second to put on and stays completely and securely out of my way when I'm not using it.

Carrier or Seat Belt

And I want to mention car ride safety. In a high-force car crash, you can no more hold onto your dog than you can hold a human child—even assuming he was securely in your arms at the time of impact. Yet many people who would never drive with an unsecured infant think nothing of driving with their dog loose in the car, or held in place with a leash through a seatbelt, or even in their lap between the driver and steering wheel.

---

[33] A properly fitted martingale or sighthound collar is also a good option for those breeds whose skulls are smaller than their necks. See the Appendix.

Besides being illegal in many areas, this is dangerous in case of impact—or even on a perfectly normal car ride. I knew someone whose puppy went quiet during a short drive home, and though she thought the puppy had simply fallen asleep, in fact the puppy caught his head between car seats and suffocated to death.

A little confinement can go a long way toward safety.

There are many options for securing a dog during a drive. See the Appendix for some of my recommendations.

Now that the scary part of the talk is over, let's go on to the fun stuff!

Let's Hit the Road

There are many places to go for socialization outings. We want to find places which are safe, fun, and typical of the human world we want to normalize for our dog.

It's important to note that any time I take my dog on a socialization outing, my priority needs to be the dog and his experience. This doesn't mean I cannot multi-task, of course; I can burn calories or play a virtual game as we walk in the park, or I can have a sandwich while we're at the outdoor restaurant, or enjoy the music at an open-air concert. But if the dog needs a break or needs to retreat, his experience takes precedence over mine. I need to be prepared to give up that 10,000-step goal, or get the sandwich to go, or head back to the car from the concert.

Most of the time this isn't necessary. But having the right mindset in advance will save a lot of frustration in the moment, and may help to prevent problems developing because you'll take breaks sooner than if you were debating.

Here are a few easy options:

- A strip mall parking lot
- A grassy park
- A wooded park trail
- Outdoor seating at a restaurant[34]
- A veterinary clinic waiting room
- A veterinary clinic examination room (no exam)
- A friend's house
- A friend's yard
- A parade or music festival (at a comfortable distance, observing crowds and music at a safe volume)
- A drive-in theater[35]

Note what is *not* on this list: A dog park.

Dog parks are typically high-energy places and often full of friendly-to-the-point-of-rude dogs and humans. A dog park is best saved for a well-socialized and older[36] dog who indicates that he actively enjoys the experience.

---

[34] A perfect place to utilize that mat training previously mentioned!
[35] These still exist in some places! And they can be fantastic socialization options.
[36] It's also a higher disease risk for young immune systems.

I usually describe a dog park visit as "clubbing" for dogs, equivalent to a room full of pumping bass, flashing lights, a mosh pit, and a line of strangers sizing up whom to approach next. While some people really enjoy that kind of weekend, other might regard that as nightmare fuel—and no one thinks it's the best way to introduce an infant to human society.

I've had many clients who worried they had unfriendly or defective dogs because their dogs did not enjoy doggie day care or dog parks. This is not a defect, it's a personality, and it's fine. Do you know anyone who prefers hanging out with a few friends over snacks and a movie instead of going dancing at bars? Congratulations, you have that personality in your dog. Despite the popular idea of dog parks as a play utopia, they really aren't fun for every dog. Don't feel bad if your dog would rather curl up with a good book, as long as he can also be comfortable and polite when he does go out.

More Sensible Precautions

Sometimes we get so caught up in the importance of socializing that we forget basic comfort and safety concerns, and I frequently see dogs on socialization outings who are uncomfortable or even in distress.

If the pavement is too hot to keep your hand flat on it for a few minutes, it's too hot for your dog, too. Be careful with summer outings.

Make sure you offer fresh water at regular intervals. A collapsible water bowl[37] is easy to carry and essential for dogs panting with heat, exertion, or excitement.

The sun is hot. If you have a hat or other protection, you may not notice as quickly that your dog needs shade, too.

And in the other direction, the cold can be brutal. While most dogs can handle colder temperatures with acclimation, the key word is acclimation, and even acclimatized dogs can suffer with extended exposure. Salted surfaces can also hurt paws, especially if broken ice has opened any tiny cuts in soft, unconditioned pads, so be watchful and careful.

Signs of Stress

Make sure to watch your dog for signs that the outing is getting overwhelming, or isn't fun anymore. We gain nothing by pushing a dog to physical or mental exhaustion, and indeed keeping him out too long can actually create problems.

Here are signs of stress to watch for:

- Panting
- Hesitation
- Wandering away
- Sniffing ground
- "Zoomies" (running in circles about handler)

---

[37] See recommended gear in the Appendix.

- Whites of eyes
- Curled toes
- Respiration rate
- Fidgeting
- Whining
- Barking
- "Spacing out"
- Loss of interest
- "Bored"
- Change in ear position
- Change in tail position
- Lip licking

Occasionally one hears advice that if a dog is agitated in an environment, the best thing to do is to keep him there until he's too tired to react any more. This may look like it's working—hey, he's no longer freaking out!—but the take-home message for the dog is one of hours of anxiety, frustration, and other emotional baggage we don't want to cart around for the next outing.

In human terms, imagine an obligation you don't want to attend—perhaps an extended family reunion, a dental procedure, jury duty. Would making that experience last even longer make you more willing to do it the next time? Not so much.

It's far more efficient to make shorter, less-stressful trips than to try to push through it and hope he forgets next time how unpleasant this exposure was.

Frequency

The rough rule of thumb for socialization is that as long as you're doing it properly — not overwhelming the puppy — there is no such thing as too much.

There is definitely such a thing as too little.

I would love to see puppies go out every day, even several times a day, until about 16 weeks old. After that, I still recommend a couple of days a week of socialization outings.

If that sounds like too much, remember that these outings don't have to be huge commitments. Are you going out to pick up the dry cleaning or a package at the post office? Fantastic, take the puppy with you. It can be that quick, often just a moment or two. Most of your socialization outings are going to be under 15 minutes, often much less.

But as with general training, more and shorter sessions are *far* more effective than fewer, longer sessions. Do not try to make up for a lack of outings with extended, tiring outings; you're only teaching your dog that going out is exhausting.

Take-Out Meals

I love this term, borrowed from Kathy Sdao. She points out that rather than feeding our dogs at home all the time, we could use some of that ready-made supply of anticipation and pleasure to **classically condition** the act of going other places with that same pleasure. So pack up the dog's meal, drive to any safe place, and get out and feed the dog.

This might be a parking lot, a gate to a park, a friend's front yard, a grassy strip alongside a shopping mall. The idea is just that going places is not stressful, nor overly exciting, it's just something nice we do. It's a great way to get a dog comfortable with going to new places.

Chapter 8 Physical Considerations

VIKING REENACTMENTS ARE FUN & EDUCATIONAL, BUT TIRING.

Puppies, especially the younger ones, generally have three distinct modes of operation: zoom, nom nom nom, and dead sleep.

As eating can take only a small part of the day, no matter how they might plead otherwise, this leaves the bulk of their time divided between fierce active play and napping.

Socialization can and should be a part of play, and mental exercise is just as important to healthy development as physical. But just as we don't want to overwhelm a puppy mentally, we don't want to strain him physically.

Puppies are generally pretty good at self-regulating. When they are tired, they flop into a patch of sunlight and fall asleep, absorbing photons to recharge and awake fresh in a blaze of exploratory chewing. (Or is that just at my house?) But when they are actively engaged with us, they will often push themselves beyond their comfort level for the sake of spending time with us and playing our games. It's very flattering, but it puts the responsibility for safety on us.

When taking socialization walks or just wandering the neighborhood, watch for signs of fatigue. Puppies have twice as many legs as we do, but they're considerably shorter, and their cardiovascular systems aren't yet equipped for long duration exercise. There's a reason wild canids stay near the den with young pups instead of traveling; puppies aren't built for long walks.

It's best to plan shorter walks that end before a puppy tires out. But if your pup slows down or stops, take a break or consider carrying him.

When I picked up Undómiel in Denmark, I booked a day for us to get to know one another before we would depart and spend 8 hours on a plane back to the USA. (I didn't want a panicky puppy in a tin can at 30,000 feet!) I knew an 8-week old pup would not be up for much walking, so I brought a puppy sling for her as I played tourist. She alternated romping beside me on her leash and riding in her sling, watching or napping as she desired. We worked out our first communication that day, as she would jump up toward the sling when she was ready for a break. It was a fantastic day of socialization and fun for both of us, and though she had not been crated before and was not a fan, she loved her new sling so much that I simply left her airline pet carrier roof slightly open so that it felt like the sling, and she rode home like a champ.

Note that I am not recommending that your dog be a "purse puppy," rarely or never touching the ground in public. He can certainly walk for himself, and it's much harder to socialize a dog who doesn't walk in a novel environment. In addition, these puppies often don't get enough exercise.

Don't carry a puppy more than necessary—but do carry when necessary.

Climbing & Repetitive Exercise

Don't ask very young puppies to do long flights of stairs; it may be hard on their joints. (A couple of steps onto the porch is okay; changing floors several times a day is not.)

Letting puppies climb on things is a great proprioception exercise and a fun exploratory activity, but letting puppies jump off those things they've climbed can be dangerous. Young bones are soft and at greater risk for spiral fractures. Make sure you either lift your puppy off the couch or his latest imaginary mountain, or provide a way for him to safely climb down rather than jumping to the ground or floor.

Puppy skeletons are incomplete; the epiphyseal plates (or growth plates, soft cartilage in long bones which will calcify at maturity) may not close and harden until 18 months of age. Until then they are more prone to injury, and a skeletal injury during development means a greater risk of repeated or related injury as an adult.

This means you should exercise some restraint with higher-impact games such as ball fetching or flirt pole chasing, especially quick turns which put a lot of pressure on the bones and soft tissues. Keep turns and stops gradual until the puppy is more mature.

I like to play with unstable surfaces with my puppies, on wobbly boards or inflated exercise balls, etc. These can be great for confidence building and body awareness, but do be careful both to prevent falls and to prevent alarm in a puppy not ready for this level of challenge. Make sure also that no paws can be pinched if the surface shifts. We want positive experiences!

Laevatein came to live with us as we were completing construction on our house. As Indiana springs are not compatible with an unfinished roof, we had an enormous tarp over our very tall house. One day young Laevatein worked out a way to climb and ride down the tarp as a long and slippery slide. She thought it was great fun— bold and fearless puppy!—and despite the height it was a very low-impact activity because of the slide. (We moved the tarp anyway, because it was too high to risk an accident.)

Most of the time puppies are self-regulating and will not climb higher or run further than they feel comfortable. But keep an eye on them, anyway. They do need to run and play and explore, for both physical and mental development—remember that even sound genetics will not be expressed without the proper environment—and free play is one of the best ways to exercise mind and body.

In short, take it easy with young dogs and physical exercise. Aside from the obvious health and safety risks, a dog who is tired or sore is not having positive socialization experiences. There's plenty of time and lots of safe ways to play.

Chapter 9 "It's All In How You Raise Them"

DID NATURE OR NURTURE DO THIS?

This phrase is most often heard as a palliative during discussion of a "dangerous" breed, assuring the listener that it's the people, not the dogs. While I am whole-heartedly against breed-specific legislation and breedist prejudice, I think it's important to point out that this well-meaning phrase does a deep disservice to all dogs, especially those whom it is usually meant to protect or exonerate.

This statement assumes all dogs are born as completely blank slates, to be written entirely by their experiences and training, and that they will internalize only the experiences and training that we desire. It's a lovely dream for trainers, but it's simply not real.

It's a mistake to negate genetic influence. Genetics do not absolutely determine behavior, of course; we have ample examples in canine littermates and human twins to illustrate that. But they are certainly an influence, and an important one. Anyone involved for some time in canine rescue can call to mind examples of dogs in absolutely horrific conditions who remained friendly and pleasant and safe to handle, and of dogs who despite an adoring family displayed suspicious, defensive behavior or severe resource guarding. These dogs were carried through their environment by their powerful genetics—some to a good place, some to a dangerous place.

We *know* genetics influence behavior, or else we would not have spent several thousand years selectively breeding dogs for varied specific temperaments and purposes.

Genetics is a complicated ball of twine, to say the least. Over fourteen thousand genes are expressed in the brain, and to say a few weeks of puppy class can cleanly overwrite all of them is naïve at best.

Environment and Genes Work Together

So which is more important, genetics or socialization? Is it nature or nurture which matters? The answer is: Yes. Or explained more fully: you can't separate them, as they work together to produce the final result.

Many genetically determined physical traits still need environmental input to activate or develop. For example, rats raised in darkness for the first 30 days of life showed morphological differences in their optic nerve development[38]. Even though the development of the optic nerve is encoded in a rat's DNA, it requires an appropriate environment to express properly. Genetics carries the code for the optic nerve, but it's exposure to light which affects whether[39] and how quickly that nerve[40] will develop[41]. Genetics do not function independently of the environment.

The same is true for behavioral traits; genetics provides the framework, but environment (including training) builds within that framework. A dog whose genetics just don't allow for suspicious, guarding behavior is not going to be able to sustain that behavior even in a hostile environment. A dog whose genetics are innately neophobic and suspicious will never learn to be relaxed and wiggly in a crowd.

This is where breed tendencies come in—and I need to emphasize the word *tendencies*. Breed is *not* a determinant of behavior. While it is true that the average Golden Retriever is not a great candidate for guarding a junkyard

---

[38] Fukui Y, Hayasaka S, Bedi KS, Ozaki HS, Takeuchi Y. Quantitative study of the development of the optic nerve in rats reared in the dark during early postnatal life. Journal of Anatomy. 1991;174:37-47.
[39] Hubel DH, Wiesel TN. Effects Of Monocular Deprivation In Kittens. Naunyn Schmiedebergs Arch Exp Pathol Pharmakol. 1964;248:492-7.
[40] Mccourt ME, Jacobs GH. Effects of photic environment on the development of spectral response properties of optic nerve fibers in the ground squirrel. Exp Brain Res. 1983;49(3):443-52.
[41] Wagner HJ, Kröger RH. Adaptive plasticity during the development of colour vision. Prog Retin Eye Res. 2005;24(4):521-36.

by night, due to their predominantly social and trusting genetics, it is both untrue and potentially dangerous to assume that any Golden Retriever must therefore be social and trusting. (In fact, resource guarding is common in Goldens.)

But within a breed or a breeding program, the genetic pool gets significantly more limited in scope. It's well documented for example that genetically fearful lines can be created fairly easily, locking fearful traits within just a few generations. The most famous example in dogs is the strain of "nervous pointers," selectively bred for fearful behavior to humans at the University of Arkansas in the 1960s and maintained for study for decades after. The fearful behavior bred true from the first generation and ever after. Intriguingly, even pharmacological intervention seemed unable to overcome the faulty genes of these dogs, with only 3 of 17 treated dogs showing even short-term benefit and none showing long-term recovery[42].

Don't panic—this is not to argue there is no use in attempting to help anxious dogs! Indeed, there's a great deal that we can do to help them. My point is that genetics do matter, and often quite a bit. Our decisions each time

---

[42] Tancer ME, Stein MB, Bessette BB, Uhde TW. Behavioral effects of chronic imipramine treatment in genetically nervous pointer dogs. Physiol Behav. 1990;48(1):179-81.

Social, Civil, & Savvy

we breed or buy or adopt have a great deal of relevance to our future life with that dog and to dogs in general.

Let's revisit a concept from *Fired Up, Frantic, and Freaked Out*: A dog's individual genetics determines the end posts of where it will sit on a given behavioral continuum. Environment—including training!—then adjusts exactly where that individual dog will rest within those genetic parameters.

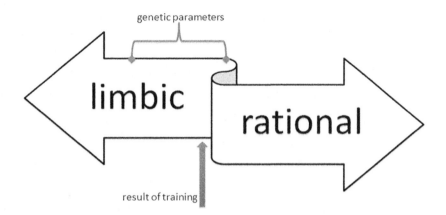

A puppy with the genes for a great temperament still needs socialization to develop that great temperament. The genetic parameters may prevent the puppy from sliding into completely neophobic territory, but it will never be the puppy it would have been with proper socialization. Likewise, a puppy with a weak temperament genetically will benefit greatly from a good socialization program, but it will never be the same puppy as one with stronger genetics.

When we say, "It's all in how you raise them," we are

purposely ignoring the genetic framework inherent in the dog. We then set both dog and human up for frustration and failure. When a single mother of three is furious that her Border Collie keeps chasing and nipping her traumatized children despite her best efforts to reinforce couch potato behavior, we suggest she's at fault or her training is bad, because "it's all in how you raise them." A Cane Corso may be deeply uncomfortable in a busy, social apartment or condo, surrounded by friendly strangers, but a well-meaning owner takes him home anyway because "it's all in how you raise them." A dog living on a chain in a backyard plays well with the visiting kids once a week and sees no one the rest of the time, and it's clearly not a problem or the dog wouldn't be safe with the kids, because "it's all in how you raise them."

Don't get me wrong, how we raise them *does* matter. A lot. It's why I wrote this book. But it is certainly not the only factor. Genetics provides a framework, which is why choosing a puppy wisely is important (and why a puppy's immediate family is a better indicator of genetic tendency than his breed). Once we've picked those genes, it's our job to socialize and train to raise the best dog we can within the framework we've selected.

Chapter 10 Preventing Resource Guarding

"PLEASE TOUCH MY STUFF.
PLEASE TOUCH MY STUFF.
C' MON, TAKE IT!"

Preventing resource guarding—growling or snapping over food, toys, space, or other resources—is not strictly a part of socialization, but it shares some common ground in that it is an important puppy subject and a subject of frequent conversation and terrible advice, which often creates the very problems it's intended to prevent. So I feel it's important to address it here.

The tendency to resource guard can be both strongly genetic and learned through experience. It's easy to see why a dog raised in a kennel with twenty other dogs and meager rations might feel the need to hoard and defend its food, but often owners don't understand why a dog raised with a plentiful bowl would growl over it. The answer in the latter case might be genetic.

Breed tendencies can be noted here, some logical (many hound breeds show low incidences of resource guarding, precisely because these dogs were bred to live peaceably together in large kennels) and others seeming to be an unhappy accident of selective breeding for other traits

(Golden Retrievers tend to be more prone to resource guarding, even at very young ages, than other retrievers). But again, it's important to note that a breed tendency is only a numbers game and not a predictor of what behaviors any individual dog will display.

Regardless, I feel that a simple exercise to help to prevent resource guarding of food is never harmful and could do a great deal of good, so let's get to it.

Bad Advice

First, here's what *not* to do: play with your dog's food.

I know, this is an extremely common bit of advice, from helpful websites to authoritative professionals, and it's one of the most damaging pieces of misinformation out there on the subject. Many people may tell you to put your hand into your puppy's bowl and toy with his food as he's eating, or to pick up the bowl and replace it to remind him that you're in charge of it, or similar actions.

Don't do this.

My strong suspicion is that this "preventative program" works only with dogs who had little to no genetic inclination toward resource guarding and were extremely unlikely to show it anyway. For dogs which might be inclined to guard their food, however, this kind of annoyance can kick that latent possibility into actuality.

My parents went on a cruise vacation a few years ago and shared an assigned dinner table with two other couples. One woman at their table, liberally lubricated from the bar by supper each night, would lose whatever inhibitions she generally had during the day, and she would help herself to food off other people's plates at dinner. "Oh, that looks good! I'll try some."

What started the first night as an annoying episode which would make a quirky story to retell quickly became a real irritant as the pattern continued. My parents are very nice people and they also felt somewhat constrained by the formal environment, and they did not slap the woman's hand or stab her reaching fingers with a salad fork. However, even their normally friendly and civil natures were strained—and without the promised relief of the trip's end, if the situation threatened to go on interminably, something drastic would have been done.

I, being fond of my dinner and not fond of rudeness, might have stabbed her with the fork. As we've said, genetics isn't everything.

The moral of this story, besides *Don't drink to stupidity*, is *Even nice personalities get tired of bad behavior*.

A dog who might start with absolutely no concerns about his food bowl might well start to develop them when his meal is constantly interrupted or taken away. Not to mention, if you are making the bowl a big deal and something to fret about, then you are teaching him that it's a big deal and something to fret about.

Unless someone has dropped a cyanide tablet in your puppy's bowl, keep your hand out of it. There are better ways.

This is a very simple exercise, intended to inspire a happy attitude in dogs without an existing resource guarding problem[43]. I think it can do a great deal to help a borderline case, and it will never hurt a case where the dog is disinclined to guard, so it's worth incorporating into any dog's life.

I don't like to wait until I see real problems before I work on problem prevention. When my Doberman Laevatein was a puppy, she was chewing on a bone, and I noticed as I walked through the room that she reversed her body position as I passed, twisting away from me so that the bone was shielded as I walked by. Now that could have been pure coincidence, and she just happened to change position just as I happened to walk by, but if she were at all concerned about me getting near her precious bone, we weren't going to let that attitude progress any further. And even if it were only coincidence, then the worst thing that happened was that Laev and I wasted some pleasant time sharing games and treats. Not bad!

Arm yourself with some high value treats, more valuable than whatever is in your dog's bowl. If your dog is eating a dry kibble, this is pretty easy—cheese, meatballs, anything more exciting than the comparatively boring

---

[43] If your puppy or dog is displaying warning signs over his food dish, such as freezing, staring, or growling, I recommend you view Lindsay Wood's much more complete Clicker Expo presentation on this subject (http://bit.ly/2lB3OIo) and consult a professional.

stuff in the bowl. I'm going to use cheese in this example, but match to your dog's needs and preferences.

Go ahead and give a full bowl to your dog, making sure that the location is dog-friendly. If his bowl is in a corner, for example, and you approach from the only open direction, he might feel trapped. We want him to feel perfectly at ease.

As he's eating, walk forward and pitch one of your super-delicious treats right at his bowl. If you can get it in, great! but if your aim isn't so good (or if his head is playing goalie), don't worry—all that matters is that the treat lands right where he'll notice it. "Cheese!" we want him to think, and then he'll probably go back to eating his kibble.

Walk away, come back, and drop another piece of cheese. Walk away, come back, drop another piece of cheese.

Repeat this until as you're walking toward his bowl, you see some sign of anticipation. He might wag his tail, pause and look for the incoming cheese, or even look up at you. Regardless, we are looking for a relaxed, happy posture. If you see tension of any sort, you are moving too fast and getting too close.

When you see some sort of happy anticipation as you approach—"Oh, boy! Here comes the cheese boss!"—then you can start holding out for a bit of engagement. You might say his name as you approach and see if he looks up at you. Then drop the cheese, as he's expecting.

If he's able to greet you with a relaxed face and a happy tail, it's time to start placing the cheese in his bowl. Walk up, reach down, drop the cheese, and walk away. This should be quick, not blocking the bowl or moving it. The take-home message for the dog is that a human hand moving toward his bowl results in bonus treats immediately appearing in the bowl, without any frustrating delays.

By this point most dogs are going to be pretty excited to see you approaching their food bowl. When you're getting the tap-dancing anticipation of "Where's my cheese?" then you can start picking up the food bowl, placing the cheese in it, and replacing the food bowl. Be quick at first, don't stand all the way upright; you're just getting the bowl into your hand and then immediately returning it in a better condition. Who could argue with that? Certainly not a cheese-loving puppy.

I like to add a little informative cue here, so the dog knows exactly what's about to happen. Predictability is a big part of comfort and safety. So just before I reach down, I'll ask, "May I have that?" Then lift, cheese, and return. This way, when I need to practice this skill in another situation, it's not coming out of nowhere and surprising the dog when I take his stuff—I have a phrase which tells him exactly what game we're playing.

If you're wondering how this is different than messing with a dog's bowl, remember that first we carefully conditioned the dog to regard our mere approach with joy, and we are watching carefully for any sign of stress or conflict. We are not just handling his food and bowl, we are carefully teaching him to *want* us to handle his food and bowl.

Gradually work up to asking, "May I have that?" and then standing upright with the bowl and then returning it, freshly loaded with cheese.

If there are others in your household, they can all practice this game, starting at the very beginning of approaching, throwing a high value treat, and leaving. Children can also practice this with supervision and careful attention to detail. Toddlers and anyone incapable of following the rules should be kept from bothering the dog while he eats, of course.

You can also start playing this game with toys, chews, and anything else a dog keeps or carries. I have with my own dogs worked up to asking them to hand me their raw knuckle bones. (I returned them with a smear of peanut butter added to the meat.)

The easy way to think about this is, *Have I earned my dog's trust with his stuff?* That is a far clearer picture than, *Have I messed with his stuff enough that he's used to it but not so much that I've sensitized him to interference?* We are reminded that this trust must be earned, it's not ours by right of having grabby hands.

Again, if at any point during this process you see signs of stress or conflict, abort. I do not want my dog to get into the habit of worrying about me approaching his stuff. Of course, if you see any signs of aggression or resource guarding, consult a professional. Dealing with a full-blown resource guarding problem is not within the scope of this book.

Chapter 11 Often Overlooked

IT'S IMPORTANT TO BE PREPARED.

It would be impractical to list every stimulus a puppy needs to encounter (although a sample checklist is provided as a guideline in the Appendix). But here are some key things which are often overlooked, either through absence of mind or lack of easy access, and how to include them.

Genders, Colors, and Fashion Senses

In our modern society, our communities are increasingly diverse. But many puppies are kept at home or in a single neighborhood, and they may not see as many types of people. Everyone's known or heard of a dog who "doesn't like men," and especially in rescue dogs this is often attributed to abuse—but it's more often due to lack of socialization, never learning to meet and read new people of different statures, vocal tones, heights, widths, and more.

As with meeting anyone, make sure the puppy is invited to approach the new person, never the new person approaching the puppy[44]. We want the puppy to make choices and feel confident in them. Follow all the general guidelines for introducing puppies and people, making sure that the puppy meets a wide variety of folk.

Children

This one can be tough, because often training the puppy is the easier half of this equation! But proper socialization to children is critical to help prevent fear and/or aggression in the future.

Again, the puppy should be invited to approach the child, and the puppy should be free to leave the child at any time. Parents should model correct behavior—if the kids are instructed to pet the puppy's back, which is a great idea, then the parents should also pet puppy's back. Parents should not hug the puppy and then expect children to show respect for the dog's personal space or comfort. Teach careful, respectful handling—no hard patting, slapping, grasping, etc. (Rule of thumb: if the puppy isn't allowed to do it to the child, the child is not allowed to do it to the puppy!)

Be sure to include children of all ages, from toddlers to pre-teens.

Bear in mind that letting an over-excited child meet a puppy does no favors to either. The puppy may be

---

[44] See the guide to meeting puppies in Chapter 4.

overwhelmed, and the child is practicing greeting behaviors which might well be dangerous with another dog. Even excited children must follow the greeting protocol in Chapter 4, allowing the puppy to approach and handling the puppy respectfully.

Nor should we include a reluctant child in a socialization encounter. This does the timid puppy no favors, and if a bold puppy tries to make friends, a frightened child's reaction can create a permanent bad impression. There are generally enough children eager to help by meeting a puppy that no reluctant child need be pressured into this role. Work at the child's own pace to acclimatize her to a puppy. Good socialization practices are appropriate for all species!

Substrates and Surfaces

Have you ever known a dog reluctant to walk across manhole covers or sidewalk grates? What about metal examination tables at the veterinary clinic? Have you known a dog who just couldn't find a place to urinate unless on grass? What about the dog who seems perfectly housetrained until the first frost or snow? All of these can be addressed in early socialization.

Ideally this kind of socialization can begin as soon as puppies begin to walk and explore. The earlier they learn that different types of surfaces are normal, the better. You need not include every possible substrate on planet Earth;

the concept for puppies to learn is that surfaces can vary, not that there is a strict list of acceptable surfaces. But more is better than fewer.

Again, the key here is to build confidence. Pressuring a puppy onto a new surface or placing him on it and expecting him to cope are not the best approach. A genetically-healthy puppy will naturally begin exploring and will naturally be curious about new textures and surfaces; our job is to make sure those experiments are fun and rewarding.

If you acquire a puppy from a good breeder (see Chapter 13), this will have been started before you ever met your puppy and you should be well on your way, but do continue through 16 weeks or longer. If you adopt a puppy from a shelter, your puppy may be primarily accustomed to concrete and blankets and little else. If your puppy came from a less conscientious breeder, it may be used to the garage or a barn or a single room of the house.

Lay out a playground of textures with carpet squares, cookie sheets, gravel, a plastic office chair mat, canvas tarps or painting drop cloths, all sorts of things. Scatter a few fun items about, a plush toy or a ball or a pine cone to sniff and taste. Set your puppy down and move around the texture map with him, letting him explore at his own pace and tossing a few tiny treats down whenever he ventures onto new terrain. We want him to figure out that walking on something unfamiliar produces treats or leads to a fascinating new toy. Puppies love this game!

Note—and this should sound familiar by this point—do not to try lure him onto the terrain with the cookies or toys. We prefer him to explore first, eat second, and we don't want him to be concentrating on the food and then startle himself by stepping onto something unexpected. Even more important, we don't want to teach him to freeze at the sight of something unfamiliar and wait for food to appear, rather than thinking and acting proactively. This is a problem created with a well-intentioned but poorly-executed use of food.

As the puppy gains confidence, upgrade the playground with moving parts—bent cardboard which flattens under a puppy's weight, or wobble boards (be sure paws cannot be pinched). Again, reinforce exploration and experimentation with praise, petting, and treats.

Advanced round: *bubble wrap*. Do not use unless you have a confident puppy who will actively enjoy discovering and controlling the sharp sounds, but this can be a great one if you do! (Note: ingesting bubble wrap is contra-indicated. Be a good puppy parent.)

NOTICE UNDÓMIEL IS WATCHING HER HANDLER, NOT A TREAT— SHE'S DELIBERATELY OFFERING BEHAVIOR WITH A NEW CHALLENGE!

Also introduce your puppy to standing water, frost, and snow. Create a shallow puddle to wade in (and then upgrade to a shallow pool). Spread some chipped ice for summer puppies to play in. Does this seem like an unnecessary effort? Ask yourself whether you want to save time during that first month of winter weather, waiting and shivering while your puppy decides if it's safe to pee in this new stuff which chills his paws. Sure, this isn't the real thing, but why not teach him it's fun to walk on cold water and icy bits now so frost and snow are less of a shock later?

What's that? You live in southern California and the weather never varies from perfect, you say? How nice for you. Do you think you might ever travel to visit relatives in New York, or take a family trip to Tahoe? Wouldn't it be great if your dog already knew how to walk in snow and take care of toilet business quickly? Or just ask yourself, When is being prepared ever a burden to yourself or your dog? Yeah, never.

Weather

Again, your southern California puppies have the blessing and curse of fine weather. But when rain does come, or when you travel with your dog, it can be quite a shock to a dog who's never really paid attention to all the stories The Weather Channel told of other regions.

Walk your puppy in the rain—sprinkles are fine, we're just after the concept. Go out in the wind and play training games. Play with your puppy during thunderstorms—many dogs don't show a fear of storms until later in life, but it's never too early to start conditioning storms to be comfortable rainy days instead of terrifying ordeals. Interactive playtime like fetch or tug is great for storms, or alternately use fun and engaging puzzle toys such as stuffed Kongs.

Young creatures of all species adapt a surprising number of opinions from the adults around them during early exposure. If you act like rain is a big deal and you don't want to walk in it, your puppy will believe you and will not want to walk (or use his puppy toilet) in the rain, either. Save yourself time and effort by teaching puppies early that weather is a variable and perfectly normal experience!

Most importantly, don't let the weather disrupt your

socialization. There's a phenomenon known among dog trainers in four-season climates as "winter puppy syndrome," a puppy who came home to his new family during the cold winter months and thus had his socialization very limited by, "We'll go out more when it's warmer." This delays critical exposure beyond the critical socialization period, and the end result is an under-socialized puppy.

If your winter doesn't allow for safe exposure to water, don't wait for spring! Introduce your puppy to water indoors. I have filled a bathtub with a couple of inches of water and floated a cupful of kibble, making a "bobbing for apples" game. I've also dumped ice cubes in a shower stall, letting a puppy chase them about the floor and experience ice and meltwater on her paws. Get creative! Teaching a puppy that water is fun, that he can control the splashes, that it's all a game, is well worth a few wet pawprints on the floor. (Put down a towel for exits.)

I do understand the dilemma of inclement weather. The day I flew home with young Penny, we left her southern California home at about 70 degrees and arrived to -14 degrees Fahrenheit. She was in shock and was not sure how she could even urinate outside, much less explore and be happy! Forget comfortable, it was not even safe to have a puppy outside for long. But I made our outside trips brief and I took advantage of every safe and dog-friendly interior location I could, and she grew up to be a dog who shrugs off both Daleks and dinosaurs.

There's a saying, "There's no such thing as bad weather, only bad clothing." While I don't entirely agree with this—I live in Tornado Alley, for one thing—I do think that we can do a lot in inclement weather if we take a little time to plan. It will be well worth the bit of sweat on a hot day or the extra layer on a cold day to ensure the dog is adequately socialized and prepared for whatever may come.

Chapter 12 Taking Care

"IF I SIT REALLY STILL FOR MY SHOT,
CAN I GET AN 'I WAS BERRY GOOD'
SCRATCH' N' SNIFF STICKER?"

*H*usbandry behaviors is a fancy term trainers and zookeepers use to describe teaching an animal to participate in their own veterinary care. It is much, much simpler to trim nails on a dog who thinks it's a fun training game, for example, than on one who is squirming or even biting to escape.

There are some behaviors and situations which I feel dogs should know and understand, regardless of how often we use them. It's like knowing how to jump a dead car battery or rock a stuck car out of a ditch—you may not need the skill every day, but when you need it, you're glad you have it.

These general veterinary and care behaviors include but are not limited to:

- Nail trims
- Crating and relaxing in a crate

- Wearing a muzzle
- Having teeth, eyes, and ears examined
- Accepting restraint
- Bathing
- Brushing and combing (if necessary for coat)
- Stripping (if necessary for coat)
- Chin target (useful for everything from eye exams to blood draws)

Most of our dogs are no longer covering miles of rough terrain every day, and so they require regular nail trims. It's a game I start with my dogs very early ("toes for treats!") and one they learn to love—because who doesn't want cookies for allowing me to touch their feet?

I knew we had it right when I could use a nail trim, where the dog feels in a control and is confident of reinforcement, to counter-condition a scary thunderstorm, replacing one emotion (fear) with another (pleasant anticipation). Boo-yeah!

The key to success is not to teach the dog to tolerate these procedures, but to teach him to actively engage in them like any other training exercise. It should be no odder to hand me a paw for a nail trim than

to "wave" that paw for a treat.

You can find a video detailing my approach to nail trims at http://bit.ly/2kXiMeW. Chirag Patel has a great tutorial on training to wear a muzzle[45] at http://bit.ly/2lbp59X. You can extend these ideas to all necessary training, teaching the dog that this is a normal and voluntary part of interaction, that it's not scary and is in fact an opportunity for games and reinforcement.

I often joke with clients that if we can train a multi-ton whale or a Siberian tiger to voluntarily offer body parts for needle sticks, we shouldn't need three people to hold down a small dog. It's all in the approach!

---

[45] You can see some of the reasons why you might want to train this even to a young dog without overt problems in my blog post at http://bit.ly/2lRk7Dk.

Chapter 13 Acquiring a Puppy

IT'S IMPOSSIBLE TO SAY NO
TO A PUPPY IN YOUR LAP.
PLAN AHEAD.

M ost of this book is for the reader who already has a puppy or new dog at home. But if you are the kind of forward thinker who obtained this book to prepare for the puppy or dog you plan to bring home, this chapter (and a shiny gold star for planning ahead) is for you.

Even with the best of intentions for training and socialization, acquiring the right puppy to train and socialize is important. Breed traits and individual personalities mean we need to find the right new family member.

Bad matches can lead to simple frustration (a marathon runner looking for a jogging partner adopts a Neapolitan Mastiff) or to dangerous situations (a family of six with special needs children who need extra attention adopts a Malinois, or a mobility-challenged senior citizen gets an enthusiastic Labrador). Everyone, human and canine, will be happier with a good match. Don't be afraid to take your time.

Many times people know they shouldn't choose a puppy solely on looks or a breed's popularity or "cool factor," but it's hard to remember these helpful guidelines when there's a warm wiggly puppy in your lap. Planning ahead can save a lot of mental effort!

Breeder or Rescue?

Let me emphasize first that there is no universal correct answer to the question of where to search for a puppy. I should also explain that I personally have adopted abandoned dogs off the street, adopted via rescue organizations, and researched for years before buying from a breeder on another continent. All three methods brought me great dogs who fit well in my household. There is not a single correct approach.

That said, there are common mistakes, and these should be avoided.

A good breeder is priceless. A good breeder will give you a puppy which is genetically sound—both in body and in temperament—and which has been well-started in a solid socialization program. Before my puppies were 8 weeks old, my breeder had introduced them to many adults and children, had built them a jungle gym of various surfaces and moving parts for climbing and exploration, had taken them on car rides and exploratory walks in different places, had introduced them to other dogs, had even taken them on walks beside an air strip! These puppies had a great start on accepting new and unusual things in their world, because it had never been limited to start.

There are a number of signs of a good breeder:

- They will tell you why their breed, and why their litter in particular, is not for everyone (careful of bad matches)
- They will require references, probably from a veterinarian and possibly from a trainer
- They will have a contract specifying that they will take the dog back if ever you cannot keep him (good breeders are very careful that their dogs will never end up in a shelter)
- They may have a spay/neuter clause in their contract
- They will not let you buy a puppy on your first contact or visit—no quick sales, they want you to be sure of the puppy and they want to be sure of you
- They often have a waiting list before a puppy is born—or even before a puppy is bred

A poor breeder, on the other hand—a "backyard breeder" in popular parlance—may make your puppy-raising more difficult and charge you for the trouble. This is a breeder who does little to no health testing to identify and prevent genetic disease or heritable conditions, who does not start socialization early and in fact may limit the puppies' exposure—and then charges more than the local shelter's adoption rates, where the puppies have the same gamble on untested genetics but usually have better socialization already.

Watch for these red flags:

- They encourage you to buy when visiting
- Puppies are kept in backyard, barn, a single room, or other isolated area
- Puppies have not met more than a dozen strangers (not breeder or family) of various ages and ethnicities
- Puppies have not left the breeder's home for socialization outings
- Puppies' parents have no health testing (including, but not limited to, OFA, CERF, and various breed-specific conditions)
- They claim healthy dogs don't require testing, or their breed doesn't require any testing

Yes, their puppies are cute, but *all* puppies are cute, and you can find a puppy just as cute but with a better chance of being a healthy, stable family member. It may feel cruel to leave a puppy behind, but it is also cruel to support the production of puppies which aren't given good starts in life[46]. **Don't pay someone to make disadvantaged puppies.** If you want to rescue, there are plenty of puppies to rescue at your local shelter, where your money goes to a better cause.

I think it is obvious to most by now that pet stores, selling

---

[46] As in all things, reinforce the behavior we want to see and don't reinforce the behavior we don't.

the products of puppy mills, are the worst place to acquire a puppy. These puppies have all the disadvantages of a backyard breeder, with the additional disadvantages of having been reared in relative isolation until being shipped out like inert product, and the breeding stock producing these puppies live in horrible conditions and are subject to all kinds of physical and mental abuse.

Don't be fooled by a pet shop saying they don't use puppy mills but instead buy from "private breeders"—all non-government breeders are legally private breeders, so that includes puppy mills. Likewise, there's a pet shop near me which advertises "100% Rescued Pets!" but declines to say which rescue or shelter supplies the puppies and kittens. Do not support these abusive companies. A purchase here is not rescue, it is funding further exploitation. Better to put puppy mills out of business by going elsewhere.

Chapter 14 It's Cool

SHAKESPEARE TEACHES KIDS HOW TO GREET DOGS PROPERLY

My Doberman Shakespeare came to me at eleven months old. I was his fourth home. I had no idea of his breeding and very little of his early life.

But I'd had him in my training class with his third owner, and he spent a great deal of time in public with me once he came to me, so he got a lot of catch-up on seeing the real world and interacting with people and dogs. He absolutely loved training and engaging with his environment. While we had to overcome some gaps in his early education—he was never fully comfortable with crutches or nail trims—he became a very stable, very educated dog.

For a number of summers, we participated in a program for special needs and at-risk children. In the space of a week, Shakespeare would meet and do demonstrations for about 2,000 kids. It was intense work for us, but the kids loved it.

One encounter in particular has always stuck in my memory. Shakespeare was lying on the ground (it was hot, and we'd put in several hours already), but still amenable to the kids' interactions. Children were taking turns petting him when one boy was brought up by his teachers. He was disabled and clearly beside himself with extreme excitement at the idea of touching Shakespeare.

Shakespeare rolled onto his side—not an appeasement gesture, just getting comfortable and exposing a side he wanted rubbed—and lay still. The little boy bent with help to reach for the dog, touched Shakespeare, and began screaming and flailing his arms with sheer joy. He lost his balance and landed on Shakespeare's outstretched ear, pinching it against the ground as he continued his enthused shrieks.

This was a situation I would *never* have deliberately set up for my dog—being stepped on and screamed at, by someone waving his arms in a potentially threatening manner. I attempted to intervene, trying to shift the boy's weight or convey to his teachers that we needed to interrupt and move him.

But Shakespeare caught my eye and, in one of the glorious moments of communication possible between human and animal, he managed to convey, "No, it's cool."

This dog, who once stepped up to confidently drive off

two adult male would-be assailants to protect me one night, lay quietly under an atypical and extreme display of emotion while his ear was pinned. He knew enough, was experienced enough, to recognize the difference in truly threatening behavior and this boy's inadvertent mistake and misdirected joy.

While I still would never ask a dog to tolerate screaming, flailing, and a pinched ear, I can appreciate that it was Shakespeare's years of experience which allowed him to make the educated decision that the boy was not a real threat.

Educating our dogs on our human world is one of the kindest things we can do for them and ourselves.

Appendix

Puppy Gear

As it would be impractical to list all items and sources here, where links might become outdated or new options might go unnoticed, I am providing instead a link to my site where I maintain and update a collection of items I've personally found useful with puppies or public training. You can find that list at http://bit.ly/2n8fVjG.

Fitting Collars

Collar fit is a safety concern, not only to keep dangerous pressure off the trachea and nerve bundles, but to prevent a puppy slipping free in a hazardous location.

For a flat collar which buckles or snaps, slip two fingers beneath the collar and slide them along the underside between the collar and the neck. They should slide easily, without a lot of pressure, but there shouldn't be a visible gap between fingers and neck.

A martingale or sighthound collar (the terms are interchangeable) has a limited tightening capability and relies upon friction and a temporary tight fit to keep a collar from sliding off a dog with a skull smaller than her neck, such as greyhounds or Dobermans. On this type of collar, the two sliding rings should come within an inch or two of each other when the collar is tightened, snugging down enough that the collar cannot slip over the dog's skull but not so much that it will act as a choke collar. Because this collar can put more pressure on the throat, it's often wider to distribute that pressure, from 1.5" to even 3" wide in a long-necked adult. I generally like the widest collar which doesn't feel awkward or interfere with the dog's neck flexion (don't put a 3" collar on a tiny puppy!).

Regardless of collar style, keep in mind that puppies can grow very quickly and it's a good idea to check collar or harness fit every two to three days during the fastest growth spurts.

More Training Resources

Are you looking for more training for your puppy? Try these excellent books and other resources.

There is no licensing body to easily separate educated and skilled trainers from the rest. Look for a certified trainer using the guidelines provided. I can also recommend any trainer found at http://bit.ly/TzSx8u, as certified trainers from the Karen Pryor Academy (of which I am a graduate and faculty) must graduate their courses with an A or not at all. There are of course many excellent trainers with other credentials as well!

- *Puppy Start Right*, by Kenneth M. Martin DVM and Debbie Martin, RVT VTS (Behavior) CPDT-KA KPACTP, and www.puppystartright.com, where you can search for a local course for training and socializing

- *Idiot's Guide: Puppies,* by Connie Swaim KPACTP
- Dr. Sophia Yin's puppy socialization checklist, http://bit.ly/TI7W5s
- www.ClickerTraining.com
- *Agility Right from the Start,* by Eva Bertilsson and Emelie Johnson Vegh
- *The Power of Positive Dog Training,* by Pat Miller
- *Clicking with Your Dog,* by Peggy Tillman
- *The How of Bow-Wow,* DVD by Virginia Broitman and Sherri Lippman
- ASVAB guidelines for choosing a trainer, http://bit.ly/2mRa4Ph

Socialization Checklist

While it would be implausible to provide a complete list of everything a puppy should experience, as this list would vary by geographic location, intended career path, etc., here is a good overview courtesy of Chris Puhls. You can download a PDF to print for your use from her site at http://bit.ly/2mGjCwb.

Socialization check list: {Exposure should be fun or at least neutral. If you see a fearful response or avoidance behavior, increase distance or otherwise reduce the intensity of interaction until the puppy/dog is happy)

Created by Chris Puls (feel free to use/share)

PEOPLE:	PLACES:	SOUNDS:	SURFACES:
Friendly interaction with:	Outside at night	Phone	Carpet (thick/thin)
Tall	Outside when it's windy	Dish Washer	Linoleum/tile/hardwood
Large	In the rain	Clothes washer/dryer	Grass (short, long, wet)
Short	Walking trails	Hairdryer	Mud
White	Open field	Coffee Grinder	Concrete
Black	Beach	Vacuum	Blacktop
Hispanic	Friend's houses	Shower	Bricks/pavers
Asian	Pet friendly business	Loud music	Rocks/gravel
Smoke/alcohol on breath	College	Dropping pans	Bark/mulch
In coats (bulky or long)	Outside grade school	Overhead garage door	Wood/deck
In hats	Retirement Center	Lawn mower	Stairs (closed riser)
In wheelchair/walker	Busy parking lots	Dremel tool	Stairs (open riser)
Crutches	Pedestrian tunnel	Screaming/crying kids	Sand
Using umbrella	Quiet party/gathering	Laughing kids/adults	Wet
Pushing shopping cart	Big city/downtown	Barking dogs	Warm
Elderly	Shopping center	Thunder/heavy rain	Cold
In mask/costume	Hotel	Shouting	Makes noise
Babies/strollers/cribs	Flea market	Singing (live)	Plastic (sheeting)
Safe kids 5-10 yrs old	Airport/helipad	Cheering/applause	Plastic (hard/solid)
Kids 10-15	Carry young puppy or wait	Sirens/Alarm	Slippery (tub/ice, etc.)
Teens	for immunity to go in:	Beeping	Uneven/rough
Veterinarian in Dr. coat	Grooming shop	Whistling	Squishy (couch/bed)
Police officer in uniform	Vet office	Whistle (blown)	Metal
Firefighter in turnout gear	Pet Store	Clanging	Grate/mesh/netting
Observe at safe and/or	Dog show/event/trial	Squeaking	Ramp/incline
comfortable distance:	Puppy Kindergarten	Shopping carts	Slide (playground)
Runners/joggers	Dog park	Traffic/Honking	Moving/unstable
Cyclists	Dog daycare	Weed wacker	Agility contacts
Skateboarding		Construction sites	High surface
Skating/rollerblade		Waterfall	Fixed boat dock
Wrestling		Cars Honking	Floating boat dock
Stationary crowds	EATING FROM:	Airplane/helicopter	Corn field pre-harvest
Moving crowds	Your hands/fingers	Echo (voices/shots)	Corn field with stubble
Crying baby	Other people's hands	Quiet popping	Stubble cut field
Angry people	Metal bowl	Air in plastic bag	Thick scrub brush
Carrying large load	Plastic bowl	Smack 2x4s together	Shallow water/puddle
Shooter (for gun dogs)	Flat plate	Balloons	Deeper water
Football/baseball team	Paper plate	Outside indoor gun range	Moving water
	Glass container	Gun range (distant)	Water with lilly pads
	Treat dispensing toy	Gun range (close)	Thick muddy water
	Kong/stuffed toy	Bird calls (different)	Pond with underwater
	Eating off of:	Bird launcher	weeds/trees
	Grass/straw	Bird splashing into H20	Salt water
	Concrete/Brick/Pavers	Real ducks/geese	Waves
	Dirt	Boat motors	Sucking/grabbing mud
	Sand	Walkie-talkies	Snow
	Water (floating treat)	Garbage truck	Bubble wrap
		Motorcycle	Aluminum foil

OTHER ANIMALS:	PLAY WITH:	CONTACT/SPATIAL:	OTHER:
Puppies of dif. breeds	You/your hands	Collar grab	Photos taken
Playful dogs	Soft/stuffed toys	Touch/hold feet	(including flash)
Friendly but aloof dogs	Squeaky toys	Touch/tap/clip nails	Practice waiting quietly in
Stern dogs	Fleece toys/tugs	Use dremel on nails	crate in several places
Dogs of all sizes	Appropriate sized ball	Touch/look in ears	Swimming
Dogs of all colors	Oversized/herding ball	Touch/hold tail	Automatic doors
Dogs with different hair	Food dispensing toy	Full body restraint	Balloons (Helium type/
Cropped ears/tail	Food stuffed toy/Kong	Gently tug on fur	squeaky sound made)
Pushed in noses	Moo tug/soft rubber	Brush all over body	Animatronic decorations
Missing limbs	Frisbees (hard/soft)	Look at/brush teeth	Stuff in the sky (kite, plane,
Deaf and/or blind	"flirt pole" toy	Take temperature	Blimp, etc.)
Playing/wrestling	Giggle ball	Hug	Person hugging puppy
Running/chasing	Talking toy	Lift/hold/carry	Person blowing air in face
Friendly cats	Light up/flashing toy	Lean over the dog/pup	
Unfriendly cats	Nylabone	Lie on side	
Rodents/pocket pets	Bully stick	Lie on back	
Reptiles	Rope toy	Gently stretch/massage	
Rabbits	Bumper (bigger pups)	Give bath	
Ferrets	Cardboard boxes	Dried with towel/blower	TRANSPORT:
Fish tanks	Plastic bottles		Car/passenger van
Birds (pets)	Crumpled paper		Truck/Cargo van
Birds (wild/waterfowl)	Chamois rag		Shopping cart
Chickens/turkeys/ducks	Soft leather rag/tug	Desensitize to SCENTS:	Flat wheeled cart
Horses of all sizes	Note: Be sure toys are	"Critter odors" for any	Wheelbarrow
Cows	proper size/hardness for	outdoor sports	Elevator
Sheep	your puppy/dog.	Critter poop	Escalator (with jump)
Other livestock		Bird scent (gun dogs)	Bus
Note: Young puppies can		Cooking food	Plane
observe other animals from		Other people's treats	Row Boat/kayak
a distance if immunity is a		Food/treats on floor	Motor boat
concern.		Dead animals	Golf cart
			Train
			Subway
			4-wheeler
			Ambulance (Service dog)

Note that this exposure should ideally be started by your puppy's breeder after the pups eyes open. So if they are not already providing you with this list, filled in with what the puppy has already experienced, you might want to share it with any future breeders you plan to get a puppy from so they can get started early with your next puppy.

American Veterinary Society of Animal Behavior (AVSAB) Position Statement on Puppy Socialization:

The primary and MOST important time for puppy socialization is the first three months of life. During this time puppies should be exposed to as many new people, animals, stimuli and environments as can be achieved safely and without causing over-stimulation manifested as excessive fear, withdrawal or avoidance behavior. For this reason, the American Veterinary Society of Animal Behavior believes that it should be the standard of care for puppies to receive such socialization before they are fully vaccinated. Because the first three months are the period when sociability outweighs fear, this is the primary window of opportunity for puppies to adapt to new people, animals, and experiences. Incomplete or improper socialization during this important time can increase the risk of behavioral problems later in life including fear, avoidance, and/or aggression. Behavioral problems are the greatest threat to the owner-dog bond. In fact, behavioral problems are the number one cause of relinquishment to shelters. Behavioral issues, not infectious diseases, are the number one cause of death for dogs under three years of age.
Additional information from the American Veterinary Medical Association (AVMA) at the bottom of this page:
https://www.avma.org/public/PetCare/Pages/Protect-Your-Dogs-Yourself-and-Others.aspx

Glossary

Classical conditioning—like Pavlov's bell predicting food and causing the dogs to drool, one stimulus is associated with another.

Classical counter-conditioning—pairing a desirable stimulus (special treats) with an undesirable (spiders) to reduce the unpalatability of the undesirable stimulus.

Desensitization—exposure to the stimulus until it ceases to be novel or stimulating; a city dweller ignores traffic noise that might bother a rural visitor.

Learned irrelevance—the ignoring of unassociated stimuli, or signals which do not convey a significant meaning; often seen when a cue is used too early, before the dog fully understands the associated behavior

Operant conditioning—the science of consequences affecting behavior. Reinforced behaviors become stronger and occur more frequently; punished or extinguished behaviors become weaker and occur less often.

Positive reinforcement—adding ("positive") something to make a behavior stronger; giving a treat for a sit reinforces sitting behavior.

Reinforcer/Reinforcement—any consequence which causes the antecedent behavior to become stronger.

Threshold—the point at which a stimulus becomes "too much" for the subject, whether inducing fear, excitement, etc.

About the Author

Laura VanArendonk Baugh CPDT-KA KPACTP has been working with dogs and horses since childhood, and she began training professionally in 1999. Laura was one of the earliest dog trainers to achieve national certification in the USA. She enjoys pursuing continuing education more than anyone

should, and she teaches regularly on behavior.

Laura is particularly fascinated by the science of altering behavior. In January 2008 Laura became a Certified Training Partner with the highly regarded Karen Pryor Academy for Animal Training & Behavior, and she returned to the Academy as an instructor, teaching certification workshops around the country.

You can find Laura at www.CaninesInAction.com and at www.LauraVanArendonkBaugh.com.

Get a free packet of training sheets and guidelines at http://bit.ly/2nPLvP9.

Made in the USA
Monee, IL
19 June 2020